Mike & Becky
Hope you enjoy
Gary N. Hicks

Losin' Ain't an Option

Losin' Ain't An Option

Gary Hicks and Pat Bush

Copyright © 2010 by Gary Hicks and Pat Bush.

Library of Congress Control Number: 2010912207
ISBN: Hardcover   978-1-4535-6080-8
       Softcover   978-1-4535-6079-2
       Ebook   978-1-4535-6081-5

All rights reserved. No part of this book may be reproduced or transmitted in any form or by any means, electronic or mechanical, including photocopying, recording, or by any information storage and retrieval system, without permission in writing from the copyright owner.

This book was printed in the United States of America.

Cover photo by:
Mike Moulton
In the Wilds photography

To order additional copies of this book, contact:
Xlibris Corporation
1-888-795-4274
www.Xlibris.com
Orders@Xlibris.com
83385

Contents

1. Up-rootin..7
2. Home Coming...8
3. Words of Wisdom..11
4. An Offer He Should Have Refused..13
5. The Path of Life 16
6. Cleanin' House..18
7. The Round-up 20
8. Realizin' You're the Prey 23
9. 40 Acres Maggots 27
10. Livin' and Learnin'...29
11. Biscuits & Gravy..31
12. 14 Year Affair 33
13. Life with the L's...36
14. Devotion...39
15. Bonding..41
16. The Great Coat Dance..42
17. Rough Mother's Day 46
18. Learnin' to Sleep Again 49
19. Grim Reaper...54
20. All White Guys Look Alike 56
21. Hearin' It Backwards 58
22. Not a Politician..60
23. Pride and Fear 62
24. Knowin' the Greatest Tool Invented..64
25. Havin' the Right Fair 67
26. Misconceptions 69
27. No Slack in the Trigger 72
28. Truly Dangerous Men are Nice Guys 74
29. Silence is Over Whelming 77
30. Picked the Wrong Line 79

31. Wind is My Friend 83
32. Stranded and Stupid 88
33. Dealin' with White Folks 91
34. Help's Help..93
35. Miss Communication 95
36. Hillbillies...97
37. Family Affair 99
38. False Bravado 101
39. Spectation..105
40. Smelled That Comin' 107
41. History Denied 110
42. Bare Huntin'..114
43. NITRM..116
44. Fame..119
45. Getting' All Wet 121
46. Nearly Missin'..126
47. Thieves..129
48. Leave the Dead Lay..131
49. Native Names 133
50. Justice Self Served 136
51. Pretty is Painful..140
52. We're All Family 142
53. Don't Eat the Mint 145
54. Success Without a Clue...148
55. Incoming 151
56. Gun Control 153
57. Mollycoddlin'...155
58. Brilliance...157
59. 24-7-365..159
60. I'm a Vegitarien..161
61. Desperate Aint Attractive 165
62. Keepin' Goin'...166
63. Drawin' the Line 169
64. Beneficial Loss 172
65. 100% American..174
66. Complaint..176
67. Standards...178

Chapter One
Uprootin

As I headed south from the Black Hills of South Dakota, the driving was some of the most difficult I had ever encountered.

It wasn't the snow or the ice on this lonely two-lane road that troubled me, it was the uncertainty of what was ahead and the regret of what I was leaving behind that was overcoming me with emotion and clouding my vision with the tears of fear I had made the wrong decision.

I had just left behind my job, the woman I loved and everything I was accustomed to en route to take over a roadhouse in the "Native Country" of the southwest.

Looking like a dust bowl refugee in my old Currier pick-up loaded with my tools, my Harley and 140-pound Shepherd dog named Chelsea. I had agreed with my father to go clean up this shit hole of a bar he had built back in the '60s.

He had leased it out when we left Arizona. I was in about the 5th grade when we left and over the years it had become infamous. The current lessee had failed to pay the rent for the last couple of years and needed to be removed. Compounding that situation was the over three dozen police calls the local sheriff had received in just the last year.

As I look back now those fears, though real, were slightly exaggerated. I was unaware at the time, that life's experiences had groomed me for what was to come. It would be the best job I ever hated and the worst job I ever loved.

Little was I to know, life in hell is hilarious.

Chapter Two
Home Coming

I pulled up in the parkin' lot on a Monday mornin' haulin' my tools and motorcycle in an old Currier pickup. 'Nother truck pulled in at the same time. They were goin' to the bar. Two girls got out on one side, two guys got out on the other side. Girls squatted and pee'd on their side and the boys stood and pointed on the other. Then they all went inside.

I thought, '*What in the world have I gotten myself into?*'

My father was always an entrepreneur, although he worked for the Government Bureau of Indian Affairs for thirty-three years. One of the first things he built was a bar between the Navajo and Zuni Reservations called Witch Well.

Life takes us in many different directions. We moved to South Dakota and left it behind. I thought for good, but when I was 'bout twenty-nine years old, he came to me and wanted to know if I'd go clean it up. The sheriff had called and told 'im there was just too much trouble out here. Too much hassle and the county was prob'ly gonna close down the bar if he didn't clean it up. So I came down December of '85 to look at the place; to see if I wanted anything to do with it. I was stuck number three man in a job where I was gonna be number three man for a long time so I was lookin' for somethin'.

I came to Witch Well 'round Christmas time. I walked in the bar and it was busy. Got me a beer and sat down in a booth, talked to the customers and watched the people that were runnin' the place.

Dad hadn't been paid rent in almost three years. One thing I noticed was that the guys runnin' the bar had a shoe box next to the cash register. One sale went in the cash register; the next four went in the shoe box. Over and over, one in the cash register, four in the shoe box. So I played a little pool and sat and watched.

The guy who was workin' for the lessee, walked up and asked, "Have you ever seen anything like this?"

I told 'im, "Yeah I've seen it like this. I've even seen it even busier."

He said, "Well, you been here before?"

"Yeah. I own this place."

He said, "No, the guy who owns this place is up in North Dakota."

"No, my dad's in South Dakota but I'm right here lookin' at ya. We're closin' this lease out."

He wasn't very happy with me. I left and went back to South Dakota and finalized. Quit my job, left my girlfriend and came back.

Had no electricity, no phones. I was here three days without lights, runnin' off candles and coal oil lamps. I rented a generator and it blew up after only three days. I called my dad and asked him to find me one. A couple nights later, Dad showed up with the generator. After goin' to bed 'bout four in the mornin' I got up an hour later, went out and unloaded a large diesel generator. I settled it in and by the time Dad woke up at seven in the mornin', I was hookin' up the wires. We had power.

I went to go in the apartment in the back. Old B&B (Bob and Bonnie), they told me they'd really cleaned it up. Well, when I opened the door, the smell 'bout knocked me down. The ceilin's and walls were black with kerosene soot. The windows were all gone and boarded over.

When I got near where their bathroom was supposed to be the smell was unbearable. I opened the bathroom door and bein' as there wasn't any runnin' water there wasn't any workin' facilities. These poor white trash that were runnin' the place were usin' the bathtub to defecate in.

One o' the first things I did, not knowin' how to git that mess outta what was gonna be my livin' quarters, I took a chain saw and cut a hole through the outside o' the wall, put the log chain to the bathtub with the bumper o' my pickup truck and drug it right out through the wall. I knew no other thing to do. That bathtub is still layin' out there in the pasture. Fifteen years later the horses finally got so they could drink out of it.

There was a backroom in the bar that was boarded up. When I went in there, there was one light bulb hangin' from a couple o' wires that were on the wall. I thought the walls were painted brown 'til I realized it wasn't. It was jist flies. Fly specs and flies. As I looked 'round, dog feces was over a foot deep 'gainst the north wall. I guess it came out 'bout six feet.

There were maggot-covered cow hides and coyote hides all inside the backroom o' the bar so I knocked a hole in that wall and went to draggin' everything out o' there. Then I went to work on cleanin' it up. I literally had to go in with a wheel barrow and shovel. Scoop the dog crap outta the inside o' the bar. This was not one trip. We're talkin' several wheel barrows full. While I was shovelin' the dog shit out I found a hearth, a six inch tall rock hearth in front o' the fireplace that I didn't even know was there. It was so buried I didn't even know it was there

We eventually built bathrooms back there and paneled and ran lights and built the back bar so people could come and go. It became a valued asset to the property. Much more valuable than ten inches o' dog shit.

Chapter Three
Words of Wisdom

As a young boy I spent many happy hours playin' and workin' and enjoyin' the atmosphere. This place once had charm. I kept rememberin' bein' eight years old here. This was the place o' my childhood. This is where I grew up. Kept rememberin' bein' a boy here and lovin' it. I was gonna make this work or else. I wasn't goin' anywhere.

Before I knew it, the first Sunday rolled 'round. The state o' New Mexico was dry on Sundays. Native American reservations, only a few miles away, were dry of alcohol. I had no idea there were gonna be eight hundred people show up here. All day long I did the best I could. I had an old roll top desk and every time the cash register got full, I jist emptied it out and threw it in the roll top and closed the roll.

My father gave me some o' the best advice I've ever gotten. He said, "These Native Americans are superstitious. They don't like crazies. They don't like to touch 'em. You need to show 'em you're crazy or they're gonna kill you."

That advice, right there, saved my life. When I came to Witch Well, these people here had never seen anybody pull somebody's eyeball out in a fight. These fighters here had never seen some o' the things I would do when I was 'fraid o' losin', 'cause a sane guy can't do those things.

'Bout half way through that first Sunday I had a bad brawl break out. Seven or eight grown men hammerin' on each other in the parkin' lot. I grabbed a sawed-off shotgun and rolled outside to end the thing.

A Zuni man named Elvis stopped me. He said, "what're ya doin'?"

I said, "I'm gonna kill one o' these sons-o'-bitches if they don't stop this."

He said, "Naw, don't kill anybody yet. It's your first day. Ya gotta give it a little more time."

He was right; I didn't have any notion o' killin' anybody. I brought the shot gun back in and we sent word to the Sheriff. My two-way radio to the Sheriffs' department was down. It was the only communication I had so I sent a guy to go git three ambulances. He drove over to Zuni and got the ambulances.

We got all the injured parties loaded up and then the party continued on. It rolled and rolled until finally one o'clock in the mornin' came. I locked the place up. Never been 'round anything like that 'n I didn't think I could do it. I knew I couldn't do it. I knew this was the biggest mistake I'd ever made in my life and I've made lots of 'em. I went back and sat down in front o' that roll top desk, opened up that roll and the whole desk was full o' money. Cash three foot wide, two foot high. Mixture o' bills. I decided right then and there I could prob'ly do this. I might have to git a little tougher but I could prob'ly do this.

I'd never seen that much cash. I didn't even know how much cash that was. I counted on into the night 'til I finally fell asleep in the wee hours o' the mornin'. I'd done a little over twelve thousand dollars that day. And it was April Fool's Day. The first o' the month. My first Sunday. I never in my life had seen twelve thousand dollars in cash let alone had it in my hands. Right then and there I *knew* I could do this.

Chapter Four
An Offer He Should Have Refused

It was kind of a lonely place without knowin' anyone, if you can be lonely surrounded by people all the time, but that's the way it was. We didn't have any runnin' water. Didn't have any flush toilets. Didn't have phones. Those were all the things I had to work on to build. I'm not the world's worst handyman, but I was trained by the worst. Me! I kind o' self-taught myself.

Over time I hired some locals who continue to be good friends to this day. We built bathrooms. We cleaned the place up and we still had our share o' trouble. The sheriff wasn't kiddin' when he said this place was wild and wooly.

Finally attitudes began to change. The customers had had control o' the bar. The customers had been runnin' the place. Well, they needed to learn this was my place. I was the one in control. It was a long hard summer with many battles. Some of 'em scary but all of 'em worthwhile. That's when I got my nickname o' "Scary Gary." Without those battles, without those brawls, and fights, I would prob'ly still be fightin' today or we'd be out o' business.

I've never been a tough man but I've always been a winner. My theory on fights is there's no such thing as a fair fight unless I win. Then it's a fair fight. Losin' ain't an option when you're thirty miles from help. You avoid 'em as much as you can but when you can't avoid it anymore you end it fast by whatever means necessary.

My first few weeks here, I would go to town and rent a motel room. Once a week in the middle o' the day, I'd lock up the bar and leave. I'd go to town and rent a motel room and make what phone calls I needed to make, take a shower and do some laundry.

I slept in a sleepin' bag on the pool table. Finally got a used bed so me and Chelsea, my German shepherd, a helluva dog, weren't sleepin' on the pool table anymore. After a few weeks more I got runnin' water goin' and got so I could take a shower here.

This place had been run by disreputable characters but it was controlled by the customers. I had to build a fence 'round the place. I wasn't used to wakin' up with people bangin' at my door or honkin' their horns. I wasn't used to people lookin' in my windows and breakin' in and stealin' shit.

The bar had run pretty much twenty-four hours a day. So those regular customers were used to comin' at three in the mornin', four in the mornin', beatin' on the door, gittin' what they wanted. That all had to change. It wasn't legal.

B&B, the couple who'd been runnin' it before had been tradin' jewelry for alcohol, sex for alcohol, 'bout whatever customers had to trade for alcohol. They were tradin' jewelry for alcohol out o' the bar for a couple of years. One day I went down to their house and knocked on their door. They were nervous as heck lettin' me in their little camp trailer out in the trees on the desert. When I walked in, they had emptied pickled pig's feet gallon jars from the bar and completely filled 'em with ear rings and finger rings and turquoise and silver that they'd stolen one way or another.

Many customers were disappointed, to say the least, at my new rules. They were rules o' law, rules of ethics and rules o' life. Those are still the same rules we work on today.

In the beginnin' it wasn't only teachin' and helpin' the customers with ethical behavior.

Anglos that lived in the area were reclusive at best, ill mannered and would take advantage of anyone they could at worst. They'd been takin' advantage o' the Zunis, takin' advantage of each other, and takin' advantage o' the bar. Part o' my job was endin' all that.

When I came out, it wasn't to buy this place. It wasn't to run this place. It wasn't to spend my life here. What my dad's and my deal was, I was to clean it up, stop the nonsense, clean it up and make it a saleable property 'cause in it's current state, when I got here, it had no resale value what-so-ever. Nobody wanted it. I worked three months paintin', buildin' bathrooms, puttin' windows in, buildin' an apartment and gittin' power and water.

We didn't have cell phones in them days. I got a mobile phone 'cause in the early days all I had was a two-way radio to the sheriff's department.

So Dad comes back down after 'bout three months, after I'd got the structure secured and cleaned. He asked me what I thought he could get out of it and I made him an offer. That rotten son-of-a-bitch took it and I've been here ever since. Haven't regretted a minute of it.

Chapter Five
The Path of Life

Most o' the things I've done in my life paid off in the long run, being totally unaware of it at the time. I worked construction and heavy equipment. I worked the door in a couple o' biker bars. I raised cows. Built fence. I'd always been a man o' the land but one winter I got laid off buildin' power lines and I got a job in a hardware store.

Growin' up a white boy on the rez, I learned to scrap a little. It helped me when I took this place over. It's a Zuni bar. There's a whole lot o' white guys out there that couldn't run this place. There's a whole lot o' people out there who don't have the patience, the compassion that I do.

Granted I have a reputation for being a little bit of a hard ass, but I also have the reputation that I will help people, too. I don't think there's anyone who lives up here I haven't helped at one time or 'nother. Multiple times if they've been here any length o' time. They don't live out here without needin me at one point or 'nother.

The Zuni people, in general, are wonderful. If I think o' how many people I have told no and compare that to how many of 'em have turned into jerks when I've told them no, hell, the whites are much ruder. Whites, Hispanics, the other races in the area are much ruder when they are denied a drink than the Zunis are. They tell me thanks more times than they call me ass hole. Hell, I know I'm an ass hole. I don't have any choice. People can call me anything you want but they can't call me wishy washy.

Ya know, I think if a guy was in this business and he was wishy washy, he wouldn't be in business long. Somebody'd kill 'im. They'd run 'im out o' business. They'd hurt 'im. I never back off from it once I decide. I never back up.

I've apologized to guys. I've thrown 'em out the door and said, "Ya know, I may be wrong but I'm doin' it anyway. This is a decision I've made." I know I've prob'ly been wrong sometimes, but I'm still here.

Chapter Six
Cleanin' House

Next thing I had to do when I took over was pay the previous lessors for their inventory. So we ran an inventory. I signed a check over to Cadillac Jack., partner to Hootch, for twenty-five hundred dollars and never saw 'im agin. Hootch showed up two weeks later and wanted to know where his money was.

I told him, "I gave it to Cadillac Jack. You need to git it from him."

Well, I don't know if he ever got his money but the bottom line was there was a new dog in town and the old dogs left.

The next thing I had to do was git a liquor license. The liquor license that was here, my father had transferred to Hootch. In the process o' transferrin' it back to me, the State of Arizona Liquor Control denied me a license. I'd gone to three different attorneys seein' if I could push one through. As I was doin' that one day, I was in the Arizona Department of Liquor Control. There was an oriental gentleman in there with two Italian pin-striped suits. Shady lawyers gettin' 'im a liquor license. That aggravated me to no end 'cause you couldn't convince me that he knew the liquor laws of Arizona when he couldn't even speak English. Ahhhh! I confronted 'em. The people at liquor control, the Vietnamese gentleman, and the pin stripes.

Confronted 'em all and told 'em, "You tell me he understands these laws. He can't even understand me and I'm callin' him a blankety-blank s.o.b."

Two U. S. Marshalls ushered me to 'nother liquor control office and they still denied me a liquor license. But I was lucky enough to hire me an attorney named J. L.

J. jist told me flat out, "You give me X amount o' dollars and I'll git you your license."

Well, I didn't have that kind o' money so I gave him some down and we went in front o' the liquor board. I sat in front at the liquor board 'cause I'm hard o' hearin'. I have trouble hearin' females at a distance and stuff.

So I said to 'im, "I need to sit close 'cause I have trouble hearin' and the women need to speak into a mike cause I can't hear 'em."

Old J. stopped the proceedin's and explained to all the ladies on the liquor board that I was handicapped and they had to speak clearly for me to be able to hear 'em. By the time he was done swoonin' 'em, they voted unanimously to give me a liquor license.

In exchange I still owed J. a bunch o' money. I'd got a high dollar belt for a low price off a Zuni silversmith so I traded 'im that belt for what I owed 'im for the bill. He's worked for me ever since.

Doesn't work for me very often, he jist takes his retainer every year, but he's still a dammed good attorney.

Chapter Seven
The Round-up

There was a wino problem. Still is to this day but when I got here there was one constantly. I wanted rid o' the winos and all the problems they caused.

The liquor salesman, name o' Billy Teams, one o' my mentors in the early days, told me, "No, no. Don't do that. Don't git rid o' them winos. Them winos'll put you in a new truck every year."

But, I wondered, *how much did they cost ya in damage and runnin' 'way good customers and all that?* It wasn't much of a decision for me. I wanted rid of 'em. I developed a program.

On Sunday nights we were busy. We were the only liquor for a hundred miles in any direction. It was wild and wooly. So Sunday evenings 'bout eight o'clock when the crowds were still big, I'd go 'round with a flashlight and I'd rattle the trees and the shed and I'd shake all them winos out. I'd git 'em gathered out front and give some old boys a six pack o' beer to haul 'em back to their village for me. We called it the wino roundup.

So I developed that as a program every Sunday night. One time I git one o' these little yellow Datson pickups lined up and the guy's gonna haul 'em home. I git 'bout six of 'em over 'gainst the fence to git in this ride. He gits a couple in the front with 'im and I'm loadin' 'em in the back o' the truck. There's a guy standin' next to me the whole time.

I keep tellin' 'im, while I'm helpin' the other guys git in the truck, "Git in the truck Bud," and he don't say nothin' to me.

I say, "Come on, Bud. Git in the truck."

Well finally I reach down and grab him by the belt and I lift. I mean he is not budgin' one inch. So I rear back and I'm gonna whip 'im in the back o' that truck. He don't budge.

I said, "Bud, what the hell's wrong with you? I'm tryin' to help you git in there."

He said, "I would, Gary, but they're parked on my foot."

They been parked there the whole time. When they drove up they parked on it. While I loaded all those other guys in the back they were parked on it. All that time, he never said a word.

I reached up and I tapped on the window and said, "Hey. Roll ahead a little bit."

He rolled ahead a little bit and I pushed the guy into the truck. He landed in there backwards. The guy revved the truck rrrrrrrr, made a u-turn and up the hill they went.

All of 'em raised up in the back o' the truck, "Bye, Gary, we'll see you next Sunday," and off they went.

One time we got some winos. I got three of 'em a ride in an El Camino and we got one in back and the other two were goin' in front. We couldn't close the front. We can't git the dammed door closed on the passenger side.

The driver starts yellin', "Close the door, Gary. Close the door"

So pretty soon I'm just leanin' on that door. I'm crankin' on that door tryin' to git it closed. Son-of-a-bitch. I'd jist 'bout git it latched and it won't latch. Ain't anyone in there sayin' anything 'cept the driver.

He was sayin', "Hurry up Gary. I gotta git goin'."

The other guy ain't sayin' nothin'. Well I open up the door and his foot is smashed between the door and the rocker panel. The whole time I'd been breakin' his right foot and he ain't sayin' a word. I thought he was lookin' at me like *go ahead and close the door*. So finally, old me, I look down, pull his foot back, stuff it down in the floor boards and off they go. That was unbelievable.

One time, them winos; I was runnin' new wire, new electric all underground. I hadn't been here very long and I didn't have the fence up, down 'round the pump house. I jist had a steel re-bar door on it that I'd found layin' 'round. It fit. It'd been on there at one time, or other, but it wasn't when I got here. So I put it back on there.

I had a big roll o' number nine copper wire 'cause I was runnin' new electric and everything underground. Some winos'd got in there and they'd fished that roll up to the iron bars on the door. They needed to unroll it 'cause they couldn't get the roll out o' the door so they'd unrolled that five hundred foot o' copper wire. It was a bunch of money. They'd unrolled it all in there when I did my wino roundup.

I'm out there and I dig two out from under the tree and said, "Hey guys, git on up." There's a girl there with 'em and she don't wanna git up. Rose, Steve Wallace's ex.

Anyway she don't wanna git up so I say, "Come on. Let's go."

She finally got up and she'd been sittin' on that roll o copper wire, hidin' it under her big skirt.

In those days you had to lock up everything. Still do, actually.

Chapter Eight
Realizin' You're the Prey

We had a guy down the road who was runnin' a little trailer park. Like most o' the folks 'round here he didn't have water. Didn't have power. After I got the generator goin' and put a pump on the well, he was gittin' his water from us. Well, one day he showed up to git water. While I was helpin' 'im git the hose up to his water trailer I noticed he had a wheel barrow in the back o' his truck. That's when I needed a wheel barrow to finish movin' that pile o' dog shit. So I asked 'im if I could borrow that wheel barrow while he was gittin' my water.

"No, but I'll rent it to ya."

I told 'im, "I don't really wanna rent it. I'll buy it or borrow it but I don't wanna rent it."

"Naw, I need to keep it so I'll rent it to ya but that's it."

Then he walked down to the bar. Well he didn't realize I'd followed 'im. When I came in he was makin' the brag he'd been gettin' free water from the bar and he'd never spent a dime in here and never would. He didn't realize I was right behind 'im. So I informed 'im that was the last load o' water he was ever gonna git. So in the last twenty years that trailer park has been more-or-less out o' business. Some people never learn not to bite the hand that feeds you, or gives you water.

We had one forty-acre-maggot name of Cora, come out from LA try to build a cabin out o' gluin' 'luminum cans together she'd picked up 'long the road. She was gonna use super glue and silicon and a calkin' gun. She had herself some plywood and 'luminum cans and she glued 'em together. Built her a shack out here.

Her son dropped her off with a load o' stuff and she built pretty much everything out o' that load o' stuff. Had an old station wagon for a while but it bellied up on her. Her idea was she cleared off a hillside on her forty acres. Side hills o' them sand dunes, there's a little brush growin' on 'em. She cleared that off and laid out blue tarps. Had blue tarps spread all over the hill. She'd dig a pit and lay it with a blue tarp. At the bottom o' that blue tarp she'd put a bucket with a screen on it. Her idea was she was gonna collect ground water 'n dew, and make ice. That's how she was gonna make a livin'.

Cora had a ice machine up there in this 'luminum shack. Now there ain't any power lines. No electricity for twenty miles in any direction. And she got her a two-thousand-dollar wood stove. Old, classic green enamel wood stove and the ice machine and that's 'bout all. Oh, yeah, she's got a two wheeled hand cart.

She came out here to the high plateau to collect dew 'n ground water in a desert to make ice and sell it. And she's fourteen miles o' dirt off the highway.

She comes in here one day. She finally gave up on ice machines. It's wintertime up here. Now winter up here sends the maggots out. She comes walkin' in 'cross the road draggin' her two-wheel cart and carryin a rifle, comes up to the bar. Wants to know if she can sell me the rifle for bus fare. She's goin' back to LA. She's gittin' the hell outta here. All right, but our nearest bus stop is seventy miles from here. I'm a long way from the bus, and I don't really want the rifle, it's a twenty-five dollar used 22 in them days. But I give 'er twenty-five dollars for it. She still ain't got 'nough money for bus fare and she's seventy-five miles from it.

I know she's got this ice machine sittin' out there in the shack so I tell her, "What do ya want for that ice machine? You need money to go back to California. What do ya want for that ice machine 'n that stove?"

She brings out the receipt for that ice machine. "I paid six-hundred and forty-eight dollars for it. Here's the receipt 'n that's what I'll take."

I said, "But ma'm, you're leavin' to go back to California'. Four hundred dollars right now would be a world o' money wouldn't it?"

"No. I paid six hundred and forty-eight for it. That's all I'm gonna take. I won't take a penny less."

She won't sell me the wood stove either. She wants two-thousand dollars for the wood stove and six-hundred and forty-eight for the ice machine and I see she can't even git off o' my front porch. Back in those days I only had a mobile phone. So I got through to her son in California and he said he'd send me the money and, by God, he did. I was surprised but I loaned her two hundred and I hauled her all the way to Holbrook to the bus. She never would sell me that ice machine or that stove.

'Bout a month later we went out there and my wife and I gathered up family mementoes 'n stuff that were in the shack and we sent 'em to her son 'cause he'd sent me the check.

Three weeks after that, I went out there and that ice machine and that wood stove were long gone. I'm surprised they made it that long. That crazy lady shouldn't o' been out here to begin with. The whole time she talked 'bout the government had put an implant in her head. Maybe they did. Maybe they did.

There were many other colorful characters.

A couple o' days later Bob Dodge showed up for work. We had an intoxicated, elderly gentleman who needed to leave so I walked over and sat down next to 'im.

Told 'im, "Bud, you had too much so you gotta go."

'Bout that time, Bob walked over, gathered 'im up and slammed 'im into a double barreled wood stove we had in the corner. Then he drug 'im over to the wall, slammed 'im into the door, slammed his head into the cement block, then threw the old man out.

Well, it made me mad. I stood up and Bob come over to me. I asked 'im, "What the hell did you do that for?"

He said, "That guy was gonna sucker punch you."

"That old man wasn't gonna sucker punch me".

"Oh, yeah! He was gonna tear you up."

I said, "Well, I'm done with you tearin' them up. You go ahead and git your ass out o' here. You're done. You don't work for me anymore."

The next day, after I fired 'im and ran 'im off, Bonnie, his wife, quit 'cause she wasn't gonna work if her husband couldn't work here. Lo and behold, like most o' the forty acre maggots out here, in those days, none of 'em ever lasted a year. So B&B. went their way and life was good.

That left me in the middle o' nowhere with no help. But it was still one o' the smartest things I ever did. 'Bout six months later Bob came back in and we were sittin' here and he was cussin'. In those days we only had three or four neighbors. And he was cussin' 'em all, that they was no good.

Finally I told 'im. "Bob, that's not the problem. The problem is it's you who're no good. It's nobody else, it's you."

He threw a big right hand 'cross the bar and knocked me all the way into the aluminum can barrel. When I come up, I come up with a shot gun. That thing's a double barrel. I shoved it up under his chin and walked him out the door. Then I called the law 'cause you have to report an act o' violence. A deputy showed up. While we're talkin' Bob had driven to St. Johns and filed a complaint 'gainst me for pullin' a gun on 'im.

Well, I let the deputy take the gun. Turns out it was registered to Bob and the barrel o' the thing cut off illegally and the gun was here when I got here. So it was his own gun that I shoved under his throat. And the police, the sheriff's department told 'im he ain't 'bout to come 'round me anymore. Thank God!

That was almost the end o' Bob Dodge. He was so bitter, that come that fall he had a Zuni buddy named A. to come in. A. sold me a deer tag but he had never turned the tag into the tribe. Old Bob had figured out that the only way to git rid o' me was to have A. take me deer huntin' and B. could shoot me while we was out there.

But I had a good friend named Ervin Wasita. He come to me a couple o' days before the deer hunt and said, "I was drinkin' with them guys and they're plannin' to kill you out there. So don't go on that deer hunt."

I never went on that deer hunt. I still got that deer tag the Zunis never even had any record that it was sold to me. I keep it as a reminder that not everybody out there who offers to help you is plannin' on doin' you a favor.

Chapter Nine
40 Acres Maggots

We didn't have very many white people here in the area, livin' out there in the trees. Those that we did have were colorful, to say the least. I call 'em all 40-acre maggots. Real reason white people were livin' out here was they couldn't fit in with whites anywhere, or else they were hidin' from the law. That was 'bout the only whites we had out here. We had several of 'em shootin' each other over diggin' up Indian ruins. They dug up seven o' the Pueblo Gods, Fetish Gods, over there off the hill

I'm not very superstitious but I can tell you this, out o' the three guys that dug 'em up, all three of 'em was dead within three to five years. Ray Scott and right next to him, what was that guy's name? Anyway all three of 'em were dead. The wife o' one of 'em lived out here a long time after he died, named Carol or somethin like that.

We had pot diggers, we had a hippy commune, we had a lesbian commune. We've got a preacher who's an ex-navy seal turned school teacher. Baptist preacher. He's been a good man and an ally for years.

We've had a Guatemalan, Venezuelan-, Mayan-, or Aztec. I don't know if you'd call her a practical nurse, voodoo doctor, self healer or earth child. I'm not sure what you'd call her. On many occasions she asked for my assistance. I assisted her and the ladies who lived with her.

One time I helped 'em out of a jam and she brought me some kind o' herbal remedy. Cold and cough remedy. A quart jar of it with juniper berries and leaves and all kinds o' stuff floatin' 'round in there. I wasn't 'bout to drink that crap but she told me it was good and she was a healer.

A medicine woman. They called their enclave Medicine Wheel. She told me if I ever needed anything after helpin' 'em out that she was a medicine woman and she could help.

I said, "Well, I don't need your help with the common cold. I take cough medicine for that. But if I get 'nother bullet can you take that out?"

Well, that was the end o' Ol' Medicine Woman. She wouldn't go anywheres near bullet wounds, broken bones or knot holes that I could occasionally get. The end o' her healin' experience was the common cold. And she wasn't patchin' up no bullet holes.

Chapter Ten
Livin' and Learnin'

I had a guy try to stab me with a bottle. I ordered the guy out the door and he had a liter bottle in his hand. Had a corked bottle o' rocket in a sack. I went at 'im at the door to throw 'im out. He turned 'round jist as I git there. Boomp, he banged his bottle 'gainst the concrete block and slammed me deep into the middle o' my sternum. Well, the bottle, it never broke so Boomp, he jist hit me with the round end. So I hit 'im with a big right hand that drove 'im out the door. I hit 'im and down he went out the door. When he hit the gravel his bottle broke.

I looked at him and said, "What are you gonna do now? Hayaaaah," and then he went to sleep.

There are many lessons you learn with men. One o' the first few lessons I learned, I had a older gentleman in his mid sixties that was on the fight. Maybe he'd been being disrespected 'count o' his age or 'cause o' his ass hole attitude. Anyhow, he was on the fight.

I didn't wanna hurt the old man so I waited 'til he turned his back to me. I wrapped my arms 'round 'im and picked 'im up to carry 'im outta door. While I'm being nice and gentle carryin' 'im outta the door, he reaches down to my hands locked 'round his waist, grabs hold and breaks my left index finger.

So I shove him on out the door and tell him, "You know, I'm trying to be nice to you. Look what you're doin' to me."

But he did teach me a valuable lesson. More valuable than any combatant. No matter their skill, strength or experience, anyone can hurt ya if you let your guard down.

Guy comes in one day, needs some money to buy liquor. He'd been fishin' all day and wasn't catchin' nothin' but mud puppies and he wants to sell me some. Some people call 'em water dogs. They look like little skinny bull heads. Grow to 'bout six inches long. They got external finger-like gills and little legs. I'm sure the water dog's some kind o' salamander, but a different kind. You catch 'em with worms, just like fish. Use 'em for bait. Too big for small fish. If you git big green ones, they're good for big bass. Trout, too, if you know where to go. So this guy comes in and wants to sell two of 'em for four dollars. I kind o' felt sorry for him. It was hot and he'd been out in the sun all day. So I gave him four dollars for the lot so he could git a beer.

He told me, "But you gotta watch out for them water dogs, though. You squat down to bait your hook, they'll crawl right up your ass hole."

Chapter Eleven
Biscuits & Gravy

Some o' the locals in town tried to shut me down a while back. People in Rock Ridge, they never liked this old bar out here and never will. And that's ironic 'cause this old bar funds their little league, and funds their 4-H, and this old bar does a lot for the community whether they give us any credit or not.

One o' the times they tried to close me down was a few years ago. I had a little fight up on the hill and it was three-on-one so it wasn't *too* little. It was pretty serious, but I got it done. A guy jist got outta prison and we'd had some trouble with 'im before. I wound up out in the parkin' lot with 'im and it turned into a three-on-one deal. So I wound up knockin' all three of 'em down by the time the fight was over. It wasn't pretty. Jist as I got it done some Mormon's drive by, right after I'd finished the brawl. I believe it was H. J.

The next day Tim, my hired hand, and me go into Rock Ridge to meet a gun dealer in there at the KKK restaurant, Katy's Kountry Kitchen. We're gonna meet a gun dealer 'cause I'm gonna buy some assault rifles off 'im. I'd made a deal for six of 'em. He ain't there yet so we order biscuits and gravy.

One o' them Mormons steps up to me at the table while I'm waitin' and says, "Did you come to town to git arraigned?"

I said, "Arraigned? Arraigned for what?"

He said, "Well, Old H. J. drove by yesterday and said you were standin' out front there with three dead Indians. You were standin' there with your pistol smokin' and had three dead Indians in front o' you."

I said, "You ignorant bastard. Do you think if I shot and killed three men yesterday afternoon I'd be sittin' here orderin' biscuits and gravy this mornin'?"

But noooo, they were serious. They'd said the rumor was all over town that I'd killed three guys, then I jist go to town and order biscuits and gravy. That's the way life is I guess. Yeah. I'm jist hangin' 'round. Gonna get me some assault rifles, 'cause hell, I might have to kill three more tomorrow.

Chapter Twelve
14 Year Affair

After I was here a couple o' months, I realized business was all jist Sunday only. The rest o' the week was quiet. I decided to increase my Friday 'n Saturday night crowds with a band.

Chelsea, my big old shepherd, her habit was when she had to go outside she'd come up and rub my leg. One night we got the band playin' and stuff. We got quite a few people. The dog comes up and rubs my leg. In them days I didn't have the back finished yet and there wasn't any back steps. Well I take her out the back door. There was 'bout a three foot drop outta the back door without them steps. The dog was used to bailin' out.

So we had the band playin' and the dance is goin' on and I walked up and opened the door and the dog bailed out. When she did there was a girl there holdin' onto the threshold o' the door with her pants down 'round her ankles and a guy lined up behind her with his pants down 'round his ankles. Well, that big old German shepherd landed right on the girl's back, slid down to the guy's navel. They've got bare asses, buckskin, blue jeans, dog and all revolvin'. They're goin' in a circle and 'fraid the dog would bite. The dog jist doesn't bite anybody 'less I tell her to. She looks at me like *do I bite 'em? It don't look like they're fightin'*.

So finally I git the dog back inside. The old boy, Merlin, he comes back in that night at the dance. The old girl, she never comes back in to dance the rest o' the night.

That dog was good 'cause she didn't like loud noise. Didn't like guys yellin' and screamin' in here. Didn't like feet shufflin'. Guy's feet shuffle when a fight breaks out. That dog would hear them feet shuffle and come right up over the bar.

One day I wasn't payin' attention and in comes a cripple. Come in shufflin' his feet and a hundred and thirty pound shepherd was right in his lap. He couldn't move his walker outta the way quick enough. He never got bit but it made me watch old Chelsea from then on with that feet shufflin'. Wouldn't let people dance shufflin' their feet.

The cops tried to arrest her one time. I was workin' up there on the diesel generator. Chelsea was layin' there. I was wrenchin'. All of a sudden I saw that dog jump up and leave. I thought *stray cat*. Then I thought *no, that dog left in a hell of a hurry*. So I looked 'round the corner o' the generator shed. She's got a guy down on the ground on his toes and fingernails. She's got 'im by his left ass cheek and she's draggin' 'im to me and he's doin' everything he can to help her.

I finally git the dog to let go of 'im. I bring 'im in behind the bar and and git his pants down. I grab a tube of neosporin and I'm fillin' those teeth marks. I'm squirtin' neosporin in those fang holes in his ass. So finally he leaves on out o' here. He's from Albuquerque. He goes to the doctor and somebody tells 'im he oughta sue me, or ought a have the dog impounded whatever.

The next day, Ike, deputy sheriff, pulls in out here. Him and I come in the house.

He says, "We need to take your dog."

I said, "No."

"Well, we got a report it bit somebody over in Albuquerque."

I said, "No it's never been to Albuquerque."

"Well, no, it bit him here but the guy lives over at Albuquerque."

I said, "OK, you got a warrant?"

The Deputy said, "No."

"You got a signed complaint?"

"Nope."

"Then you ain't takin' my dog."

"Well, we gotta take 'er."

"No. You ain't takin' my dog,"

"Well, we gotta impound 'er for rabies."

I said, "No. You ain't impoundin' anything. I'll keep the dog here. I'll put the dog in back and you guys can come and check on 'er.

Now the dog didn't like uniforms. So every day, Ike drove out to check on the dog. I had put 'er in the back livin' quarters. I'd open the door and Chelsea would see that uniform and bare her teeth and growl.

He'd back up and say, "Yep. That's that dog alright."

They never did take my dog. Oh yeah, old Chelsea was a good dog. She always seemed to be so gentle to most people, but in her reign here, she was a fightin' son-of-a-gun when it was necessary. She must o' bit at least a dozen guys.

Chapter Thirteen
Life with the L's

I went through thirteen employees my first year. I had quite an education on the bar business, on dealin' with cash, on dealin' with alcohol. I'd finally fired everybody who was here when I came out, and I was workin' seven days a week all by myself. I'd heard of a girl that I'd competed in sports in high school with her brothers. I'd known the girl. She'd lived in a neighborin' town when I was in high school so I'd known her for a while and I'd heard she was in Phoenix lookin' for work.

So I locked this place up one day and drove all the way to Phoenix to find that girl. Dixie. I found her and she was more than willin' to come work for me. But there was a hitch in the thing. She had an ex-navy girl friend named Sue. After Sue was here a while we nicknamed 'er Rambolina.

Sue came up here dressed in full camouflage 'n double side arms. She refused to tend bar without a pistol. Those girls worked for me for 'bout a year. One time, includin' Debbie, whose now my wife, I had three women livin' here with me.

One day the deputy sheriff pulled up.

He said, "Gary, they're all talkin' in town. They can't figure out how you're livin' out here all alone, in a one bedroom apartment with three women. Just how are you doin' it?"

I said, "I don't know, but I do know I'm tired all the time."

They took that to heart. They thought I was serious. So the rumors began to grow. Dixie and Sue were good help, but you can't put three women in the same kitchen and expect 'em to git along. It jist won't work. That was the end o' their workin' for me.

Dixie and Sue and I remain friends still to this day. Dixie was the kind o' barmaid that met you one time and remembered your name nine months later. Dixie never forgot a name. It was amazin' how she picked up on names. I been in this business with customers for twenty years and all I know is Bud or vodka tonic. I don't know their names. Dixie knew their names the first time she met 'em and never forgot 'em. I always admired her for that.

One summer I had my thirteen-year-old boy stayin' with me. Dixie and Sue were takin' a bath in the apartment. Now this boy, the only thing he knew 'bout lesbians was what he saw from *Penthouse* magazine. And lesbians, in general, don't all look like those in the *Penthouse* magazine. So we come walkin' in one day and they were splish-splashin' in the bathtub. Old James eyes got big as saucers. We walked out into the bar and I could tell he had many questions 'bout what was goin' on.

Debbie looked at James and told 'im, "This is what two lesbians really look like. Not what you've been jackin'-off to in *Penthouse*. This is what two lesbians really look like."

I think it crushed the boy. I think he had the thought that all lesbians were super models. Well he realized they weren't from that point forward. But he did have questions on why his father, known to be a conservative would allow that.

The only way I could answer that question was, "That's their business. What they do at work is my business. What you do afterward is your business. I try not to git in the middle of either o' that. I never tried to get in the middle o' them either."

One time Sue threw a fit. We had a Halloween party and she came in full military regalia. Side arms, hand grenades, the whole bit. I wouldn't let her tend bar and dance and enjoy the Halloween party heavily armed as she was. So I made her take off the heavy artillery.

At one time durin' the night Sue was dancin' with Ronnie and Ronnie flipped her while they were dancin' and she hit in a pile in the middle o' the floor back there. Her pistol hit first but she had unloaded it for me so the pistol hit empty. That was prob'ly the luckiest thing I've ever seen 'cause all o' that five-foot-tall, mad, lesbian was ready to shoot everybody in the place. That was just part o' Sue.

While I was livin' with those three girls, one day Sue and Dixie and Debbie were talkin' and I was kind o' listenin' in.

Dixie said, "I feel sorry for Gary. He doesn't have any male friends. He's with just us three girls."

Sue said, "Well, what's wrong with me? He's got me."

She was upset 'cause those girls were upset 'cause they thought she wasn't man enough to run with me. Well Sue may have been a bull dyke but she damn sure wasn't a male friend. But that's jist the way Sue was. She was a gas. You either loved her or hated her. She was a good girl.

CHAPTER FOURTEEN

Devotion

Debbie has been a part o' my life for many, many years and prob'ly always will be. She was Sales Director for Howard Johnson's. Company cars, company credit cards, skirts, and panty hose every day. When I left South Dakota, I'd left her too. She said she wouldn't come down here *until*, or if she *ever* came down here, this place had to have television, telephone, flush toilets and electricity. All these things were things I didn't have. So I went to workin' on the place and 'bout seven- or eight-months later Debbie decided she'd come down and try it for a while.

Well she did. She left the company car, her airplane flights all over the United States, and came to the middle o' nowhere to work in a honky tonk that in those days was on the edge o' wild. It was quite an education for a little Mormon girl from Pollyanna Avenue. She has done well over the years. To this day she's still an integral part o' the bar whether she works here or not.

Ninety percent o' my business are ethnic peoples. Native American peoples. Debbie was a long-haired blond, green-eyed girl from Idaho. She'd never seen anything like this before in her life. She'd grown up in a very sheltered life. Oh, she'd let her hair down in college a little like we all do. But to take a former South Dakota State Snow Queen out into the desert, out into the rough and hard life, I had concerns whether she'd make it. Whether she could do it.

Like most difficult jobs, they're highly rewardin'. The harder the job, the more you get out of it when you're successful. After leavin' Howard

Johnson's as sales director, Debbie worked side by side with me, seven days a week, for fourteen years. I never thought she'd make a week. Then I never thought she'd make a month. After a year I began seein' changes, not for the bad, not for the good, just changes. From being such a sweet, naive young girl within a couple o' years she was as hard as a horseshoe nail. She, still to this day, can cut you in half with nothin' but a phrase. And that has been one o' her valuable assets.

To survive in America there are two ways to go through life. You let life pass you by, or you face it head on and you enjoy every minute of it, good, bad or ugly. Debbie has accepted that harder road. And that makes me proud. Not that she has become a hardened person but that she has left naivete behind. Left behind the choice to let life pass her by. She faces it head on every day and that's all you can ask of a person.

Chapter Fifteen
Bonding

One o' the first friends, one o' the first men I hired, one o' the few friends I still have to this day, was named Russell. He started comin' 'round. He noticed I had a cute little black motorcycle parked out front from time to time. He wanted one so he started comin' 'round. Finally he bought him one, but when Debbie first moved here she didn't know he was my friend and she'd never seen Russ before. One day I was back in the office workin' on books. Russ came in and asked for me.

Debbie, in her not so subtle way opens the door to the office with Russ behind her and says: "Hey, your scuzzy biker friend is here to see you."

Russ and I have been friends ever since. We've helped raise each others' children. All o' his boys have worked for me from time to time. There is richness between us. If a man dies with five close friends he is truly wealthy. I don't have those. I may have many people show up when I die but as far as close friends, I guard my heart tightly. It's not easily given and Russ has a hold in it. We'll see each other to the grave.

Chapter Sixteen
The Great Coat Dance

One o' Russ's best stories was The Great Coat Dance. The Great Coat Dance began on a hot summer afternoon. Back in the days, on Sunday, when Russ was workin the door for me, we had an ex-con come in. An African American man who'd just been released from prison. He showed up at the door with an attractive Navajo girl with him. Russ asked 'im for an ID and the man wouldn't produce an ID for Russ. I showed up 'bout the time the man was gittin' aggressive.

They didn't have even a driver's license. She had a passport but he didn't have anything. The guy was 'bout six-foot-three. And he's givin' Russ hell at the door. I ain't got time for this. I walk up there and jist shove his ass out the door. Then I came back in. Well he kept at the door and kept givin' Russ hell and stuff so finally I walked out there from behind the bar.

"Bud, jist git the hell out o' here. You got no ID. You got no business bein' here. Jist git the hell out o' here."

He started callin' me names and whatever else and he's gonna kick my ass. So I threw a big right hand. When I threw that big right hand, I missed 'im by a foot. I brought it all the way 'round and that big black guy leaned back and I missed him by a foot and a half. AHWOOO! I gathered nothin' but air. He went to swingin' and poppin' and we went at it. You handle things quickly so I threw the man out the door even though he did outweigh me about fifty pounds and was taller than I was.

There are no fair fights. In them days I had gas pumps out there and we went at it all the way 'round them gas pumps. I couldn't reach that big sucker and he kept throwin' them bombs at me. I started kickin' 'im in the knee. I'd go away and bob and weave and fake with a right hand and I'd kick 'im in the knee. I'd come in and fake a left jab and I'd kick 'im in the knee. 'Bout the twentieth time I'd kicked him in the knee we were already past the gas pumps. Comin' back here that knee finally buckled on that big tall sucker. He dropped to one knee and I stepped in and gave a big right hook and put his lights out. Boom, he hit right on his face.

There were four girls right out here in a little Ford escort.

They all jumped up with their arms in the air and yelled, "Touchdown."

The whole parkin' lot was watchin' the brawl, ya know. So I come back in the door and I'm blowin', the adrenalin's flowin'.

I go into the cooler to cool off and Debbie opens the door and says, "Gary, he's back."

Somethin's wrong. You don't knock a drunk out cold and he's back in a minute. That jist don't happen. So I git to the door and there he is givin' Russ hell agin. I shove him on out the door. Out we go agin. We go and go and go and I git my shirt torn off in this'n. Finally 'bout fifteen minutes into the second brawl, BOOM, down he goes agin. By now I'm bleedin' a little bit and I'm havin' less fun all the time. I come back in and I go back in the cooler.

Debbie opens the door and says, "Gary, he's back."

I git to the door and the guy's tore his Levi jacket off and he throws it on the ground. My bouncer jumps in the middle o' his jacket and he's shakin' his big old ass and he's grindin' his jacket into the parkin' lot.

He's goin', "Come on, hit me. Hit me."

He's grindin' that jacket into the ground and this big tall black guy is goin', "I want that little mother fucker. I don't want you. I want that little mother fucker."

Russ says, "You leave that little mother fucker alone. He's gonna hurt you, bad. You hit me."

So finally I step up there and I've got an ironwood night stick. I step up there and I grab Russ and I push him outta the way.

I said, "Alright. I'll handle it."

I wrap that big ex-con up side the jaw with that ironwood night stick. He staggers back and says, "What'd ya do that for?"

This's been goin' on for over a half hour by now, ya know.

So I turned around to Russ and said, "Oh, I'm not gonna need this."

I throw him the night stick and me and the other guy go all the way out onto the yellow line in the highway. So when I finally finished it out there on the yellow line I got ahold o' him by the hair. I've had enough now. I just beat his head off the highway 'til he quit wigglin'. I grab him by the feet and I drug him off the highway. Right as I drug him off the road, Bachu Art, one o' my regulars, comes staggerin' up there drunk as hell.

He looks down at that guy layin' on the ground and says, "Now don't you come back or we'll do it all over agin."

I look back at Art and I say, "We? Where the hell *you* been?"

So then I'm teasin' Russ 'bout his dancin' and I said, "I've *never* seen moves like *that* before."

Ever since that fight we've called it the Great Coat Dance.

As slow as the law is you have to notify 'em of any act o' violence. So I call the Sheriff's department. Sheriff's department comes out and I give 'em an act o' violence report.

I said, "You go tell that son-of-a-bitch the next time he comes down here he's goin' to jail after he gets outta the hospital 'cause I'm gonna mess 'im up the next time he comes back here."

I'm still hot, but I don't realize the guy's an ex-con. Just got out for rape. He was only let out for 'bout a month before he was back in jail. He shot a couple guys the next week. He shot the bouncer at the Roundup. Anyway, so our Sheriff's department goes up there to talk to 'im.

They come back and they said, "Gary, what'd you hit 'im with?"

I said, "Well, I hit 'im with the highway."

They said, "We've never seen a black man with two black eyes before."

I said, "Well did you tell 'im what I told you to?"

They said, "Yeah, we told 'im. You still got that chunk o' ironwood don't cha?"

I said, "Yeah. I still got it."

They said, "Well you keep practicin' 'cause he may be back."

But he never came back. 'Bout a week later he shot up Lee's Liquors 'bout seventy miles up the road. 'Bout two weeks after that he shot up the bouncer at Roundup at Gallup. I never got 'nother chance to git him. But ever since then it's been The Great Coat Dance. If you've ever seen my bouncer, in those days Russ had about a hundred pounds of ass on him. Yeah, he was a pretty heavy boy in them days. He was out there shakin' that ass like nothin' you've ever seen.

Chapter Seventeen
Rough Mother's Day

One o' the bad parts 'bout livin' out here in the middle o' nowhere, I'm the first one called when there's a wreck on the road. By the time my youngest boy was four years old he'd seen a helicopter land in his front yard three times and haul bodies out. So I go to a lot o' wrecks. There've been some famous ones. We had a Mother's Day Massacre. That was pretty famous. We lost seven in that car wreck.

At the Mother's Day Massacre one o' the vehicles was a truck. So I'm sittin' inside a red Ford truck and we couldn't git the two, the driver and the passenger, out of it. We couldn't git the passenger out the passenger side. Broken pelvis, broken legs, broken ribs and we can't git the door open. It's caved in. We can't git the doors open. The driver's name's Brenda and Brenda's head is split from right between her eyes, all the way up to the top. Well it jist keeps openin' up. I had done all I could for the dead and dyin' layin' on the ground so I git me a roll o' duct tape and crawled in that truck with Brenda.

So I'm in the truck with Brenda and I tear strips o' duct tape and I put 'em up on the roof and I got 'em wrapped on my arm. I try to pull her face together, her forehead together and wrap my arm around it and hold it together and take the duct tape to try to tape her forehead together. While I'm doin' it, I got duct tape hangin' out of my mouth, and duct tape hangin' off the ceilin' and I got my hand 'round Brenda's head and I'm tryin' to hold the scalp together.

We got some white girl shows up in a silk skirt. Got a split, silk skirt on and she shows up there, out in the middle o' nowhere at this wreck. Evidently she was a nurse.

She's running 'round yellin', "I need an IV. I need an IV."

I tell her, "Lady, we're doin' the best we can with jean jackets and duct tape. Either help or git outta the way."

The Highway Patrol sticks his head in the window and says, "Are you a certified emergency medical technician?"

And I said, "No, Bud. I'm jist doin' the best I can with duct tape. You wanna help?" and he turned 'round and left.

I never saw 'im agin for 'bout an hour. In fact, he left all these injured people alone.

So I git ol' Brenda taped back together and we git over on Hagger. Hagger was over on the passenger side. We broke two handy-man jacks tryin' to git the door off the truck. The helicopters were landin' by now. We were haulin' bodies out by now. There ain't no way to git Hagger outta that truck. The whole front end's smashed in and his pelvis is broken and his leg is broken. He's broken up from the armpits down.

After we git the door finally torn off the truck, we git the gurney up there next to it. There ain't any way to git in there, git 'im up, and git im on the gurney. So finally we moved the gurney away from the truck far enough to git my body in there and then I slide my arms under Hagger's broken body and he's screamin' and cryin' and I don't blame 'im. I'm thinkin' it had to hurt like hell. Then I picked 'im up in a sittin' position and git 'im out o' the truck and turned 'round and laid 'im on the gurney. And to this day Hagger's still one o' my better customers. I see 'im every week.

Poor old Brenda lived two years and then died o' the hanta virus. I spent an hour keepin' her alive but that was it. She cleaned out a camper at Sheep Camp and came down with the hanta. It's fast and very few survive.

But I'll never forgit, in all that chaos, a registered nurse yellin' that she needs an IV in the high desert in the middle o' nowhere in a split silk skirt and a highway patrolman askin' me if I was certified or not. Well, now after twenty years the highway patrol all thinks I'm certifiable.

There's very little that's humorous 'round a wreck. But a couple I'll never forgit. One was down the road a little ways. There's an S curve and three Apache boys rolled a truck on it early one mornin'. One of 'em comes runnin' in the door covered in blood. He'd run two miles to git here. So I gathered 'im up and gathered my gear. Went to the wreck. When I got there, one of 'em was layin' on a grave that's already there and his head's cut all the way through on one side. He's missin' his right eye and his right ear and there's a big hole in his skull. I didn't know if he was dead or alive or what to do.

When I come up on him he's lookin' at me with that left eye I wanted to see if I could git a response back from him.

Maybe one of the dumbest statements I ever made. I looked into that left eye and I said, "Are you okay Bud?"

Darned if he didn't answer me and he said, "Yeah, I'm okay. Am I gonna die?" And I didn't tell 'im any diff'rent.

There was McDonalds' napkin and trash spread all over from the wreck. And I didn't have, usually I carry sanitary napkin pads and stuff for the wrecks, but I didn't have any with me. So I gathered up all the McDonalds' napkins I could find and I filled the hole in his head where his eye and ear used to be. Then I wrapped a towel around it, tied it up as tight as I could and we waited for help. Well, help finally arrived and we got 'im outta there. I never thought I'd ever see 'im agin. I figured he'd be dead. I never thought he'd make the long trip to Albuquerque.

Darned if a year later he didn't walk in here with just one eye, one ear, and said, "Are you the guy who helped me out down there on the S curve?"

"Yeah, that was me."

He said, "Well thanks. You saved my life."

Which was kind o' neat. But I still grin when I think o' that stupid question I asked that son-of-a-gun. *Are you all right Bud?* Well half his head is gone and I asked him *'are you all right?'* and damned if he didn't answer me.

Chapter Eighteen
Learnin' to Sleep Again

Over the years, I've scraped up more bodies than I ever wanted to. I didn't sign up for that job I jist got it 'cause there's no one else to do it. Yeah. Jist by my bein' the only civilization for miles. In the old days I didn't sleep. After I'd scraped one o' them bodies off the road, I wouldn't sleep for days. I've become more hardened. I sleep now.

We had one last year. The sheriff's department called in on the scanner that there was a guy stabbed at Witch Well and they were sendin' ambulances. Well, there ain't nobody here.

A neighbor called me, "Gary, the sheriff's department's on its way 'cause o' the stabbin'."

I said, "We ain't got nobody."

I finally figure out its four miles down the road. I git in the truck and I drive down there and there's a guy layin' there. I walk up to 'im and I know 'im. He's from St. Johns. There's several people who've crowded 'round now and so I interview witnesses.

They indicate to me that when this one guy pulled off the highway up to the gate that the victim had staggered up to 'im sayin' that he was stabbed. Then the victim had fallen face down and was still layin' there in the same position. I knew the guy and so I tore the back o' his shirt off and put my ear to his lungs to see what I could hear. His breath was even and clear. There was no gurglin', no bubblin'. There wasn't any puddle o' blood. I've been 'round a few stabbin's and shootin's and stabbin's bleed. Bad. Knife wounds bleed profusely. Wasn't any blood, wasn't any puddle. Bein' cautious 'bout movin' the victim with unknown injuries, I slid my hands underneath 'im and I never came up with any blood. So finally I rolled 'im over.

'Bout that time the sheriff's department and ambulance had arrived right after I rolled 'im over. So I finished tearin' the rest o' what was left o' his shirt off so I could see the wounds. See what I needed to do. I finished tearin' his shirt off. There was an Exacto knife layin' there on the ground that the witness had indicated the victim told 'im that was what the perpetrator had used. I looked at the Exacto knife and there wasn't any more blood on the end o' the Exacto knife than if you'd been scrapin' the top off a pimple. So I tore his shirt off and I looked at his wounds and he had five or six little scratches. Had a couple on his chest and one on his cheek.

Well, I been 'round a lot o' death and violence and that didn't come near to anything havin' to do with anything. He'd gone through a few layers o' skin but hadn't even broke into the meat. J. W., the head o' the Apache County Drug Enforcement Department pulled up next to me. I jist told 'im the guy wasn't hurt. I put my hands in the air and walked away. I was frustrated. I was mad that I had gone through all this for nothin'.

J. comes up to me and says, "OK Gary what's the story?"

I said, "I don't know what the story is but I don't have time for bad actin'. And that's all this is. Bad actin'."

I got in the truck and drove away. Our county went to the expense o' haulin' this guy all the way to the hospital with minor, superficial, self-inflicted wounds.

His wife came to my wife at the house the next day and said, "I want to thank Gary for all he done to save my husband's life."

The guy never got a single stitch. Not a single stitch and had cost the county untold amounts o' money, time and labor and my personal frustration. But I don't really matter in them deals. The whole point bein' you never know what you're gonna find. You never know what you're gonna run into with one o' these wrecks.

One mornin' I got up early. I was goin' to the south end o' the ranch to check water for my cows and there was a Monte Carlo gone off the road durin' the night. I see this car slammed down by the fence. Some kids were millin' 'round so I pull over and there's a bunch o' kids there. There's a half dozen at least.

"You guys need some help?"

"Yeah."

I looked at their car and told 'em, "Alright, I'll go git a chain. I think I can pull you outta there."

I come back 'cross the road and git a log chain and go down there with my truck and turn it 'round to back up to 'em. I git out o' the truck. One of 'em walks up to me and holds out an onyx chess set, a buck knife and a set o' binocs.

He said, "Here, Mister, we'll give you these for helpin' us out."

I said, "You sorry little sons-o'-bitches. That's my stuff."

Well I bought the chess set in Mexico. And the buck knife and binocs, the last I knew was in my camper. So after they'd wrecked durin' the night, they'd broke into my camp trailer 'cross the road and stole all my stuff outta my camp trailer. Then they offered to pay me with my own stuff.

Well now I'm hot 'cause I'm the only help these little bastards got in miles and here I was the first one there to help 'em. I start chewin' 'em but you can't chew on kids now like you did twenty years ago. I started tellin' 'em how stupid they were that I was the only one that could help 'em.

Nowadays they'll jump you. And that's what happened. One of 'em gits mouthy with me and a little fight breaks out. As the first three charged; I smacked one of 'em. I threw the first punch and I was gonna throw a bunch more. I'm too old for that nonsense and 'specially with several young boys. I started gettin' over-rough so I made my way to the pistol in my truck and I jerked out a big old Luger hog leg and they gave up the battle. That ended the fight. One of 'em was twenty-three, one was twenty, one was nineteen. The others all looked a little younger.

I said, "You guys rob me and then attack me? You're gonna learn a lesson from me."

So I backed back up here at the bar and called the law and the law, the sheriff's department shows up. Them kids scattered through the trees and we got us a man hunt goin' on.

Well this is all blow-sand country. You can't hide from me out here.

I git the sheriff's radio and my megaphone I use for my yearly give-a-ways party and I fire up my four-wheeler and head for the trees and we jist track 'em down.

I yell at 'em, "Alright kids. You can't hide. I got your track. You might as well come in. There ain't no way you can git away out here, ya know."

Someone yells, "I got one rounded up over here."

Somebody else, "I got three of 'em over here.

"OK. We got two over here."

We git 'em all rounded up. Oh yeah. We git 'em all rounded up and brought back.

Right away one of 'em claims that I had assaulted 'im and he wants me arrested. I think his last name was Cepto or somethin'. Well he was a sorry little son-of-a-gun and I didn't realize he was wanted by the law already. So they took 'im to jail in St. Johns. He told the officers I'd struck 'im several times. Well I hit 'im once, good, but I hadn't struck 'im several times.

The officer informed 'im, "Had Gary struck you several times you would be bloody, battered and bruised. So I don't believe that Gary beat the hell outta you."

Them boys shouldn't o' been doin' this. They had some girls with 'em. The girls were fourteen and fifteen and they shouldn't o' been out all night with 'em. So two o' them boys were hauled off to jail in Rock Ridge.

The day they got outta jail, me and Russ are out in front. We're weldin' on a trailer. Debbie's 'round too, I think, somebody else is 'round. They dropped 'em out front here so they can ketch a ride, hitch hike. They git outta that car here and they gotta walk by me. Well, the little one that run his mouth, the first one that I nailed, he goes by struttin', all 130 pounds. Twenty-one year old wannabe goes struttin' by me and Russ so we drop what we're doin'.

We stand there and tell 'im, "Come over here youngun, come right on over here. We'll help you quit that struttin"

Now, before he'd been real aggressive. Makin' all kinds o' threats 'bout what he was gonna do to me. Have sex with my wife and my dog 'long with everything else. Well, after he got outta jail he was a hell of a lot more humbler. His buddy who's with 'im tells im to knock it off and they both keep walkin' jist as fast as they could walk on up over the hill. He walked on by here walkin' to Zuni without sayin' 'nother word

I figured somewhere down the road I'd git to smack this little bastard good. But the Zunis pick 'im up. Now I may have a cruel sense o' humor in life. When he gits back to Zuni they snatch 'im when he gits to town. Not only is he wanted in Zuni for breakin' into the old folks home and a school, he's also wanted in Albuquerque. So they inform him he's goin' to jail for a while. They're gonna transfer 'im to Albuquerque to face state charges. Well, he hangs 'imself there in jail in Zuni. which may have been the easiest way out for 'im 'cause Los Lunas was gonna be no fun for that boy. So there is justice in life. It may not happen immediately, but usually somewhere down the road you git what you got comin' to you. You git what you give.

Chapter Nineteen
Grim Reaper

There's been lots o' wrecks out on this highway 'n for some reason people seem to think the bar is responsible for all of 'em. I'm not sayin' none of 'em were our customers here at the bar, but a much higher percentage o' the wrecks don't have anything to do with this place. It's travelers goin' down the road havin' a heart attack. People runnin' off the road, over correctin' and rollin' their vehicle, or ice 'n snow in the winter time. They used to plow the road. Now they don't plow the roads anymore 'cause the state has cut back on budget. Ah, very few o' the wrecks are actually involved with anyone from the bar. But the general attitude in the area is the bar's to blame.

Every time I called somethin' in to the sheriff's department was because, before cell phones, I was the only communications for miles. It always hit the newspaper headlines: *Wreck at Witch Well, Murder at Witch Well.* It always hits the newspaper as Witch Well. It may be twenty miles from here but it hit the papers that it happened right here. A lot o' stuff happens out here, but my reputation has grown far faster than my actual experience has.

My daughter was stayin' here with me one year for the summer. She was 'bout fifteen then. That same year, New Mexico had a primary election. Their bars were all closed and the reservations are always dry. So all of a sudden it's a Tuesday that's like a Sunday and everybody's here.

Our local deputy stopped by. There're two or three winos layin' under a tree. While one o' those winos was layin' there in the shade, nappin' down there; the other buddies of 'im had tied his shoe laces together. Figured when he got up he'd fall on his face and they could laugh 'bout it. Well the deputies stop by and talk to 'em. One o' the deputies, a young officer on the force, reached down and cut his shoe laces apart 'cause, well, the deputy figured the old boy was asleep. He reached down with his pocket knife and he cut his shoe laces. Then they git in their patrol car and drive off.

'Bout five minutes later one o' them winos comes up and says, "Gary we need help. There's somethin' wrong with Willie."

So I go down there, ya know. He's deader'n a door nail. He's stiff as a board. He's done pooped his pants. Life was gone. Well I'm sure life was gone five minutes before when the deputy reached down and cut his shoe laces. I come back in and call the law.

They said, "Well, hell. We're just down the road you know."

"Yeah, you are."

In them days all I had was jist a radio with the sheriff's department. That was my only communication. So I called and they turn 'round and come back.

That Deputy said, "Well, he wasn't dead when I cut his shoe laces."

I told 'em, "That's it. That was probably the only thing holdin' him together. When you cut them laces it was all over. He just bled out right through them shoe laces. It killed him. That was it."

Well it kind o' shook my daughter up a little bit. That was the first time she'd been 'round a dead body, 'specially someone she'd jist been talkin' to the night before. Took her a while to be able to sleep at night. She wasn't used to things like that. Nobody ever gets used to things like that. I'm much harder than I used to be. When I used to have a dead one I wouldn't sleep for days. Now I go home and go to bed at night so I've gotten a little more used to it.

Chapter Twenty
All White Guys Look Alike

One time I had a young couple from Australia come in. The girl was just absolutely drop dead gorgeous. This was early nineties. Quite a while back. But the girl detracted so much from her beauty 'cause she had half a dozen pierced earrings in each eye brow. She had her cheek pierced. She had 'bout a pound o' iron and stuff all over her. She was absolutely gorgeous without that shit. But by puttin' all that stuff on, there was very little attractive 'bout her to a guy like me. Now the young guys may like that stuff.

Sometimes you try too hard in life to be different. Well different has always come to me easy so I never had to fake it. I'll never forget that she was a good lookin' girl. She really ruined it.

I've sold T-shirts to people all over the world, Japanese, Finlanders, Germans. I've been in prob'ly forty or more videos.

We had a three-Japanese-wreck one time. Ran through the stop sign out there. Tourists. One little Japanese girl and two guys. And Gary Tomada and I'd been pushin' cows all day. So I come walkin' out in my old tater-chip straw hat to help 'em and these Japs take one look at me and the cameras start goin' off. And I can't understand what they're sayin. Oh, and at the time, I had a big Fu Manchu mustache. They're goin' Ken Kotta, Ken Kotta. Well it turns out they thought I was Kevin Costner and they took pictures. They must o' taken a whole roll or two. Then they went out and got their video camera. They thought Kevin Costner was tendin' bar in the middle of the desert.

So we go git four or five Zuni guys. We git their car outta the ditch. We git 'em back up here and these Zuni guys are fallin' apart over this little Oriental girl. These guys are in heat. So they're posin' with her takin' pictures. Finally Clifton gits 'er on his lap while they take pictures but he won't let her up off his lap. Finally I had to go over and separate 'em. These Japs, they didn't speak any English and I could tell they were a little nervous 'cause Clifton wouldn't let her go. He had a hold and he wasn't lettin' go, ya know.

Well darned if those tourists didn't go back to the village with Kay, my old cowboy partner. They went back and stayed in the village and stayed all night with Clifton, my barmaid. Yep. And came back in the next day and then stopped three years in a row, all the way from Japan. Darndest thing. Three years in a row they came to Witch Well 'cause they had such an excitin' time after their wreck so for the next three years they showed up agin jist to see if Kevin Costner was still workin' here. But I couldn't understand what they were gittin' so excited 'bout. 'Cause all of a sudden they're pointin' at me and snappin' cameras at Ken Kotta, Ken Kotta. That must o' been right after *Dances With Wolves* or somethin' you know. *Wyatt Earp* or one of them movies he did. And therefore there goes the basis for my theory, *all us white guys look alike.*

Chapter Twenty-One
Hearin' 'It Backwards

Comin' out o' the closet doesn't mean the same thing to everyone. Amongst the Native American people there has always been a certain amount o' homosexuality. It's always been accepted more than maybe in the rest o' society. I have several good customers that are homosexual 'cause this is one o' them tourist, Indian, red-neck, biker, gay, kind of out-in-the-middle-o'-nowhere bars. We take every body.

Well, we have a homosexual customer come in one day, havin' a few beers and the bar was lined up with tourists. White folk. And the gay man started talkin' 'bout how he had admitted to his family that he was comin' outta the closet.

He said, "My family had never realized until this week; when I came outta the closet."

Well every tourist in the bar, looked on him as bein' gay when he walked in the door. So when he said he came outta the closet, all the patrons in the place assumed he had admitted he was gay. Everyone in the bar realized he was gay the minute they saw 'im but he bragged he'd kept it a secret from his family for many years. Well, the conversation gets funnier and funnier as it goes 'cause I knew he was talkin' 'bout alcohol. He'd been an alcoholic and he was tryin' to quit drinkin' and he'd told his family he was comin' outta the closet on being an alcoholic. He's talkin' 'bout alcohol and everybody else in the bar is talkin' about homosexuality.

Finally I commended him on comin' outta the closet, and facin' his problem straight up and I wished him the best o' luck. When he left, the tourists in the bar asked me how in the world he had kept it hidden from his family for so long.

I said, "Well it's easy to hide that you're an alcoholic."

Well, they'd thought he was hidin' the fact that he was gay. And he was one o' those individuals that he *couldn't* hide the fact you know.

This gay individual had stole a purple and yellow mirror off my wall. One night, they pulled up at the drive-up window and I saw the mirror in the truck. I jist reached out the window and drug him up out o' the car window slapped him a few times and shoved him back in the truck. Trouble was he'd come to give me back my mirror and he handed me my mirror.

But life comes back to bite you in the butt. He wound up being part o' the tribal government and comin' back to haunt my ass and has haunted me for years since that.

There are many prejudices in the United States. There are many prejudices here where we live. In this bar there are few prejudices 'cause we hate everybody. We can have a Mexican, a white, a Navajo, a Zuni and a black man and when the black man leaves everybody tells black jokes. When the white guy leaves, everybody tells white guy jokes. When the Navajo leaves everybody tells Navajo jokes. So prejudice is here but here it's out in the open so it's not a big thing in our lives. Homosexuality has never bothered me 'cause I'm not interested.

My homosexuals over the years have been my best behaved, my cleanest, my most polite customers out o' the whole group. I don't run a gay bar but I would much rather have ten gay guys in here than ten red-neck-bikers. I would much rather have ten gays in here than ten Navajos. Because o' the difference in people.

Yeah. No. We don't let gang bikers in here. Yeah. I heard a bunch of 'em went to Zuni but they never made it out here.

Chapter Twenty-Two
Not a Politician

Here's my theory on solvin' the national debt. We've got prob'ly ten- to twenty-thousand men sittin' on death row 'cross this U.S. All we do is feed 'em, pay for their lawyers, pay for their medical care and pamper these guys on death row.

I say to end it all; what we do is, we cook one every Friday night on pay-per-view. We have a Friday night pig fry and we take 'im out and cook 'im on pay-per-view TV and charge $59.95. Every TV in America will pitch in and light up and they'll be orderin' it up on the internet. I'm tellin' you, crime'll go down; murders'll go down.

If you're gonna cook 'im in front o' the world, murder'll go down. We're gonna save money on lawyers. We'll save money on medical care. We don't have to house and feed these guys. If ratings start to slip or somethin' then maybe we can give the murderer to the victim's family for three minutes before we cook 'im. Yeah. Yeah. Jist tenderize 'im a little and ratings'll go back up.

Or we could do like Castro did, we could empty our prisons and send 'em all to Cuba. Seventh Day Adventists won't like it but they won't be the target audience.

That's like that show *Cops*. The only reason I watch that show is 'cause I know most of 'em. They have Albuquerque and Phoenix on there. Whenever they're lookin' for someone on *America's Most Wanted*, they find most of 'em in Phoenix. All they have to do is set up road blocks when he does his show 'cause that's where they'll git 'em all.

We got one in Springerville, last year or so ago. There was a woman who'd killed two or three. She was tendin' bar in Springerville. They had her on *America's Most Wanted*.

Somebody says, "Hey! I know her."

CHAPTER TWENTY-THREE
Pride and Fear

We've had two or three over the years. I avoid 'em. I believe everyone in America ought to avoid 'em. Nowadays men don't settle things. Years ago when men had problems they settled things.

Nowadays there's so much fear in this world that men don't settle things anymore. Nowadays they do drive-bys. Nowadays they slash tires. Nowadays they make empty threats. It's far more dangerous now than maybe any other time in history.

We have a generation o' young people who have only known despair. Have only known drugs, poverty, and abuse. They have no respect for themselves or human life. Prison may be the best thing that ever happened to them. Square meals, a roof over their head, medical care, dental. It's a brave new world but it may be more dangerous right now than it was in 1873. People hold grudges now. They used to have a fight with a ball bat and tire iron then they were the best o' friends. Nothing's ever settled anymore.

One o' the biggest changes 'round here has been our law enforcement. Years ago everybody knew everybody. We'd talk to each other face-to-face to work out what problems we had. Mainly since Bill Clinton's bill that put in 175,000 new officers 'cross the U.S. with the new breed o' law enforcement, suddenly we have that we are no longer citizens. We are suspects. The new breed o' shaved head, gung ho, Kevlar vests, ready-to-shoot law enforcement is not good for this country. It's not safe.

Granted there are those who say that's the only chance we have in solvin' the drug problem. We ain't gonna solve the drug problem no matter how many young shaved head, gun totin', ex-gang members you put out in the street. Our law enforcement used to be here to protect and serve. They're no longer here for that. Our law enforcement now is a money-makin' organization with the drug enforcement programs and others that are makin' the profit off the drug trade. Our law enforcement profits heavily off the drug trade.

I don't have the answers for it, but I know I'm no longer comfortable approachin' a police officer for help or for a question. And that is a loss all over America. We're no longer at ease with our police officers. The next step is Marshall Law and this will not do well for our country.

We're kind o' spoiled in America. We've had the greatest country in history. Accordin' to us. We've got the greatest nation in the world. Accordin' to us. Well, we're jist over two hundred years old. It's so wrapped in its own self, in its own glory, they have stepped away from the protect and serve.

Granted they have a dangerous job. There's no way I want a job where I have a domestic call every night o' my life. There's no way I wanna do that. Granted they have the right to be guarded. But not everyone out there is out to hurt 'em. A very, very small percentage o' people of America would raise a hand against a police officer. But yet, a very large percentage of police officers are more than willin' to raise hell against a citizen. I used to know every officer on the beat. Now you can't git the young officers to even wave atcha on the road.

The only reason we're still a country is 'cause of us as a private citizen. No other country wants to invade America, not 'cause we have the greatest army in the world, not 'cause we have the greatest military in the world but because the average American is armed and willin' to die for his country. Willin' to fight and die for this country.

When we become a police state and the police are no longer under our protection, we'll die as a country. We're well under way, unfortunately. A few years back they were talkin' 'bout delayin' the national elections. If they had delayed the national elections for any reason they've won. The terrorists have won without firin' a shot. If we send our boys over there to the Arab countries to die for their right to vote, aren't we willin' to die for our right to vote? Yeah. I am. They don't need to stop that vote for me. I'd be down there at those polls no matter what. Anyone wouldn't go and face the danger then we shouldn't send our boys over there to Iraq.

Chapter Twenty-Four
Knowin' the Greatest Tool Invented

I had a guy come in one time and I wouldn't serve 'im so he was gonna kill me. That's how stupid some people are. He was gonna go git his gun and kill me 'cause I thought I was John Wayne.

"You're a racist son-of-a-bitch. You think you're John Wayne. I'm gonna kill you." So he goes out the door. I'm standin' in the drive-up window and I'm lookin'. He's got an easy-rider rifle-rack in the back with a shotgun in it.

I think, *no he can't be that stupid.* So I follow 'im out the door and he walks up to his truck, opens the door and starts grabbin' that shotgun and pullin' it outta there. So I closed the door on 'im 'bout five times. I beat the shit out o' him with his own truck door. Then I took the shotgun away. I've still got the shotgun. He never came back for it. He was gonna shoot me just 'cause I wouldn't sell 'im any alcohol.

There's strange people in this world. Strange people. Alcohol is a terribly addictin' drug. I've grown up with it my whole life. My father was a closet alcoholic, a binge drinker. I'm an alcoholic in that I will still drink to git drunk occasionally. Anybody that plans to git drunk is an alcoholic. Anybody that plans to drink to excess, in my opinion, is an alcoholic. Jist like all drugs, alcohol is a dangerous thing, the things it does to people.

Our laws in this country are twisted with the dram-shop laws in that I'm liable for what somebody does if I sell 'im alcohol. I sell a guy a jug o' whiskey. He goes all the way home, gits in a fight with his wife.

Drinks half o' that jug o' whiskey, throws it on the seat with 'im, pulls out in front of a school bus with his truck. They can sue me.

Why can't they sue the company that made the truck? Why can't they? They're the ones that sold 'im the truck. That's what he did the killin' with. I'm not sayin' they can win but they can still do it. The law has come to me over cases where I might o' sold the guy the booze two days before.

I had another one. One time I had a regular come in here with a stranger I didn't know. There were three or four old cowboys sittin' at the bar. The one I didn't know was wearin' a Malcom X cap. There was a couple o' old timers sittin' at the bar.

When the new patrons walked in, one o' the old timers looked over at 'em and said, "How you boys doin' today?"

Well the second guy in the door was o' African-American descent. Right away the guy with the Malcom X cap took offense to bein' called boy. That wasn't the case. Wasn't any wheres near the case. The old rancher wasn't callin' 'im a boy, he was just askin' how they were doin'. It escalated. Threats were made. He went to runnin' his mouth 'bout it and I told 'im he had to leave. He was callin' me a racist and everything else and he told me he was gonna kill me. Gonna shoot me. Didn't say he was gonna kill me.

Tells me, "I'm gonna shoot you."

He pulls up his shirt and I could see the butt o' his pistol stickin' out the front o' his pants.

He grabs for his pistol. Well, when he grabs for his pistol, he couldn't git a hold of it. He shoves it down the front o' his pants. So he's standin' in the door and he's got his forearm all the way down into his pants leg and he's bendin' over lookin' down his pants tryin' to git a hold o' his pistol and the pistol's slid down damn near to his knees. Now he's still tryin' to git it. He's got his arm down the front o' his pants and he's bent over there by the door. So I pull Baby out.

He hears me say, "Go ahead, pull it out. I'm gonna kill you where you stand."

He looks up and his eyes git big as saucers 'cause I'm standin' there with Baby, my Colt 45, pointed at his head and the stupid son-of-a-gun reaches for it agin. I mean he's never pulled his arm out, but he goes to tryin' agin to git a hold of it. I slam a forty-five into the wall right next to his head. He looks up at me and my ears are ringin'. His ears are ringin'. Everybody's ears are ringin'. Forty-Five caliber pistols aren't meant for indoor use ya know. Things freeze for a split second and I slam another 45 round in the wall next to 'im. He dives on outta the door.

Lionel, the guy who brought 'im in, runs on out, "Oh, I'll take 'im Gary. I'll take 'im."

They git in the car outside to take off. I guess they had some trouble between 'em later was a story I heard.

Oh, yeah. There's bullet holes behind that picture over there by the door. That's why I lowered the picture. I knew I couldn't match that paint 'cause this paint was 'bout ten gallons o' different colors I threw together to make this color to have enough to cover. So instead o' tryin' to match the paint on this whole inside o' the place where I mixed 'em all together and that's what I painted the inside o' this with; I mounted that picture down low to cover up them forty-fives.

And, uh, so, maybe that was one o' the funniest gun fights I've ever been in. If it wasn't the funniest, at least it was the shortest. Poor old boy reached for his gun and all he got was a handful o' dick.

CHAPTER TWENTY-FIVE
Havin' the Right Fair

Cat fights are to be avoided at all cost no matter how high their entertainment value. Oh it happens now and then. I remember a couple.

The entertainment values of all cat fights are not equal. One less entertainin' cat fight happened one time right outside the door. At least for me. There was three girls tryin' to drag another one out of a car. I tried to avoid 'em, but I liked these girls, The Southside Girls. So I git in the middle. Two of 'em were on the driver's side o' the car tryin' to pull her out. One of 'em was on the passenger side tryin' to push her out. That poor girl in the middle was gittin' beatin' and battered.

I slowly and carefully wedged my body in between the car door and the driver o' the car. The two ladies had hands full o' hair and were whalin' on her. So, as I wedged my body in between the combatants tryin' to dislodge hands full o' hair and hands full o' clothin', one o' the smaller girls backs up and kicks. Right as she kicks, she hits me right in the crotch. I braced my hands against the top o' the car. Her eyes got big and so did mine. Every girl in the fight froze. I don't recommend breakin' a fight up that way, but it worked.

One time we had three sisters that had a problem with another woman 'cause she was messin' with one o' their boyfriends, or husbands, or somethin'. They caught her down here under a shade tree next to the tavern and the fight was on. We were busy on a hot afternoon and I was waitin' on a customer at the window and here comes a girl buck naked runnin' 'cross the parkin' lot in front of us with three, big, old mean girls chasin' her.

It wasn't that bad of a cat fight, but it was darn sure entertainin'. They had worked her over and stripped her naked, runnin' her in front o' the crowd. She hits the highway runnin' as hard as she can. Starts up the hill. A pick up fires up and runs up there, flings the door open and gives her a ride. I don't know if this theory's true or not but I assume it is and that's the reason it came up on me instantly. That was, *it don't take a naked woman long to catch a ride on the side of a highway.*

Chapter Twenty-Six

Misconceptions

I hired a bouncer one time named Scott. He was a tough guy 'cordin' to him. He'd worked here 'bout a week. I had an ex-con show up that was trouble. Him and 'nother guy decided that they were gonna start a fight up on top o' the hill. When I git up there those two were pickin' on a guy and I git up there to break it up. So the two of 'em turns on me and I ain't bashful. I went right to work and I got the two combatants subdued. Beat down and ready to leave is what I got 'em to doin'. I turned to walk down the hill and my bouncer was there.

After I'd whipped these two men by myself, I said to my bouncer, "Where the hell were you? What were the hell you doin'?"

I walked toward the end o'the bar and as I walked along he said, "I didn't know I was workin' for Sugar Ray Leonard."

I said, "You *ain't* workin' for Sugar Ray Leonard. In fact you ain't workin' here anymore, period."

I was a little bit insulted by my tough guy bouncer by makin' that statement that he was workin' for Sugar Ray Leonard. Hell. I had a bouncer that was 'fraid of a five-foot-eight bar owner. So that was the end o' his job. I figured I needed me a genuinely tough man. Not just a false tough. There's a lot o' false tough out there.

I fired him and I hired Tim, his brother, who didn't have a reputation as a tough guy. Worked for me for five years. Most dangerous man, and still to this day, one o' the most dangerous men I've ever known. I never saw him fight much, but a dangerous man don't have to fight much.

I had a psychiatrist one time doin' a psychiatric evaluation on me for Arizona. His theory on me on the first page o' his evaluation. He said, "Exhibits a stereotypical masculine facade." I asked him if he was gay. I'd never heard of a grown man who used words like stereotypical masculine facade, so I figured he was gay right off the bat. But he's probably right. I have a genuine soft heart and a lovin' kind spirit. I avoid altercation at all cost. So maybe I act tougher than I actually am.

I think, in my line o' work, I have no choice.

When I had my last gun fight, I called in the sheriff's department, "Shots fired! Need help."

It was forty-seven minutes before the first deputy arrived so that 'stereotypical masculine facade' that I put on is what keeps us all safe and alive out here in the middle o' nowhere.

Tim and I had a ragin' brawl goin' out in the highway. Six or seven men fightin' and I charged from the front door all the way to the highway. When I git to the first one, he turned to hit me. I hit 'im in the bridge o' the nose runnin' full speed. As the second one turned, I hit him and they were both down. The third one I got close to, I hit and kicked twice before he went down. The fight started breakin' up. Two turned to run from me and I was still mad. I still wanted to whip 'em all. So I ran up the hill behind them.

As they ran down the road, I was yellin', "Git, git, git, git, git, git" and they ran all the way over the hill and plumb outta sight and we never saw 'em again.

I turned to come back down to the bar and there was bodies layin' in the road. There was my bouncer cradlin' a man with his head in his arms and the whole front o' the man's face was broken. There was bone showin' and the cartilage of his nose was missin'. We didn't realize, at the time, that it was buried in my fist. I was mad and the adrenalin was flowin'. I walked by my hired hand who was gently cradlin' this victim o' the brawl.

I yelled at 'im, "God dammit, Tim, I hired you to knock 'em down, not to pick 'em up. Git your ass back in that bar," and I walked off to call for ambulances.

I had to git a couple ambulances 'cause it was a nasty brawl. We wound up needin' a couple ambulances. The ambulances arrive and no one was seriously injured.

I still see that guy today and I feel a little bad 'bout that floppy, waffle, pancake thing he's got as a nose but he did that to himself. We all learn lessons. I can reach up with my left hand and touch my nose on my right cheek. So my nose has takin' some damage of its own. There's no way you battle for a livin' and win every fight. I've lost a little bit in every battle I've ever been in.

I broke my hand in that fight. Tim and me, we sat here usin' a razor blade and we took part of a guy's nose out o' my hand. The cartilage out o' his nose was wedged between the knuckles o' my hand. So we sat here and we dug it out the best we could and then over the night my hand swole way up and the red stripes showed gangrene was settin' in.

We had an old doc, I think his name was Hamblin, in Rock Ridge. So I go down to Rock Ridge to the doc and he's in there workin' on my hand.

He says, "When'd you do this?"

I said, "Yesterday."

"Why didn't you come in yesterday."

"I was busy."

It was Sunday at Witch Well, ya know. I didn't tell 'im why I was busy. I was at work.

He said, "Where do you live?"

"Witch Well."

"Oh. I had two guys come in here yesterday. They were beat up with a baseball bat out there at Witch Well."

I said, "No doc, you're fixin' that baseball bat right now."

Chapter Twenty-Seven
No Slack in the Trigger

One time I had three Navajo gentlemen that were gonna work me over. One of 'em had a brick, but I had a can o' Bear Stop. As I approached 'em, they split out to get the angles on me. The first one charged me with his brick. When I saw him hold the brick up in the air ready to throw it; I ducked my head and ran at him full speed. He threw the brick and missed; went over the top o' me.

As I git to 'im I jumped up right in front o' him and said, "Gotcha!"

I sprayed 'im right in the face with the Bear Stop. Down he went in a pile. The one on my left charged and so I sprayed him and down he went in a pile.

I turned to the third one and I said, "It's your lucky day. I'm gonna let you drive these two ass holes outta here." He didn't want no more to do with me.

That's happened a couple o' times. We had three Vatos come in from L.A. and one of 'em was lookin' for trouble. I had to take his beer away from him. So I come up and went to pull the beer out o' his hand and he wouldn't relinquish it, so I jist crushed it in his hand and beer flew everywhere.

The fight was on. I drove 'im with both hands underneath the pool table. He went in and hit in a pile. Hit on the back o' his head and it dazed him. The big one charged and he and I locked up and we battled all the way to the door. When we got to the door I shoved him hard and there's a step goin' down out the door. He went out backwards and slapped the back o' his head on the gravel parkin' lot outside.

So I turned to git the third one and I got a hold o' him and spun 'im towards the door. As I spun 'im towards the door the other one come back in and they met face to face. KA-WHACK! And out they went. I turned 'round to git the first one that had started all the trouble. When I git to him, he's startin' to struggle to git up. But his head's underneath the pool table.

I reach down and I git him by the front o' his shirt and I go, "Come on Bud, I'm gonna help you up."

Every time I pull on 'im his face slams into the bottom of the pool table.

So I jerk him agin, "Can't you see I'm tryin' to help you. Come on. Git to your feet."

I slammed his face into the bottom o' that pool table prob'ly eight or ten times before he quit wigglin'. I drag him out and I throw 'im in a pile. By now the big one's recovered and he's outside tearin' his own shirt off, showin' me his physique. Tellin' me what all he's gonna do to me. I come back in, git my trusty can of Alaskan Magnum Bear Stop. I go out and fog 'im with pepper spray 'til he's layin' on the ground cryin' like a little baby.

Them three Yahoos got back into that compact truck. All of 'em battered, bleedin' and bloody smellin' like pepper spray and mace. That had to be a terrible ride back to L.A. They had to have a tough ride back. But some red necks are better jist left alone. But the crowd sure enjoyed me tryin' to help that guy up, 'cause every time I tried to help 'im up he'd jist slam his face into the bottom o' that pool table. I tried and tried. It never did work for 'im.

Chapter Twenty-Eight
Truly Dangerous Men are Nice Guys

I had a bouncer work for me. Tim, that I still love to this day. I've mentioned 'im before. He's made a career in law enforcement since he left me. When I first met 'im he was a Kentucky hillbilly, long hair and a *Z Z Top* beard. He come out to trap coyotes. One o' the best trappers, hunters o' men I have ever met. A talented dope grower in his day that showed promise with a lucrative future.

He's gone on with life and set aside the whims of a young man and is now heavily into law enforcement. I'm sure a wonderful officer 'cause we did everything illegal we could do when we were young.

He treats people with a compassion and understandin' that many law officers today who've had very little practical experience in real life don't have. But I think it's quite ironic that one o' the deadliest, one o' the nastiest, one o' the most contriving individuals I've ever known turned into one o' the best cops in the business.

Tim got married. Married a party girl here out o' the bar. I tried to recommend 'gainst it. My wife tried to recommend 'gainst it. We all tried to recommend 'gainst it but those of us who are in love will not listen to anything. That's not a fault. It's jist a trait we all have.

It was a tumultuous weddin' and, uh, marriage, to say the least, and it finally ended one day. They were livin' in a town nearby in a two level house. Split level house. He'd already told 'er to git out. He'd already kicked her out 'cause he couldn't put up with her drunkin', lyin', cheatin' ways anymore. So he'd kicked her out o' the house.

One day she showed up with a nine millimeter pistol. She capped the first one off when she came through the front door. It didnt' do nothin' but warn him 'cause he was upstairs not exactly knowin' what was facin' him, but knowin' it wasn't goin' to be pleasant. He quickly slips on his kevlar vest as she comes up the stairs hammerin' rounds into the house. He dives out the upstairs window wearin' full body armor. His wife is cappin' 'im through the wall as he dives out. I guess that was the end o' the marriage.

He lived to tell about it and he's much wiser since the trouble with that old party girl. She still comes 'round. She's in her fifties now, prob'ly. Still a party girl. Once you teach one o' these girls to party they never quit. Once a girl learns to party they very seldom quit, unless somethin' so tragic happens to 'em they learn their lesson. It's been my experience most o' those tragedies have been life threatenin', cripplin' or emotionally damagin' forever.

Tim's gittin' close to marryin' agin now. I'm hearin' he's datin' a Mormon girl over there in Zuni, or in Ramah. He's close.

Tim was an amazin' shot and I'm sure he still is. I have shot and used fire arms since I was eight years. I'm an accomplished big game hunter. An accomplished rifleman. But Tim was a step above. One time I saw 'im shoot a runnin' mule deer, big buck, big heavy three hundred pound buck with a thirty-thirty lever action. He jumped the deer up out o' cover and the deer was runnin' through the trees. Tim fired five times at that buck before he crumbled. This mule deer was on a dead run gittin' away from us.

We went over to secure the animal and gut 'im out 'n skin 'im. As we were processin' 'im we jerked the hide off 'im and he had put all five o' those rounds in a circle on a runnin' animal at a hundred yards and greater distance. And he'd hit that buck all five times. *In a three inch circle.* That's shootin'. Thats some shootin'.

I also saw 'im shoot a coyote with a pistol at over two hundred yards with a twenty-two magnum revolver. Set it up, took aim and whomped that coyote out there over two hundred yards. With a twenty-two mag pistol.

You can tell I love and respect that man but part o' that story is I would never go 'gainst 'im with a gun in his hand. The reason I say he was one o' the most dangerous men I ever knew is when he was in his early twenty's he read every book, every magazine, everything he could, on how to make homemade explosives. On booby traps. On every way you could kill your quarry without bein' there. He learned and studied well and he taught me a thing or two. That's why I say he's truly a dangerous man, "cause paybacks are a mother and I'm sure Tim would be capable of a very horrific payback. Still don't mean I don't love 'im.

CHAPTER TWENTY-NINE
Silence is Over Whelming

We got a forty-acre maggot, moves in out here by way o' New York, or New York by way o' Florida, to here on the desert. He'd been livin' out here 'bout six months or a year. He shows up here one day and says, "I can't sleep anymore. Somebody out there fired up a generator and I can't sleep anymore."

I talk to the local ranchers. And he talked to 'em and the nearest generator was 'bout two mile from 'im. On a clear night you *can* hear a diesel generator runnin' two miles away, occasionally. He complained all night. Called the Sheriff's department. That generator was keepin' 'im awake. Well, the owner had hauled the generator in for repairs. It wasn't even there. He called Salt River Project to see if maybe they were runnin' a new machine down at the power plant almost thirty miles away that was keepin' 'im awake. He called the Navajo Nation 'cause he'd heard that they had the Peabody Mine up at Dog Town. Their giant shovels were keepin' 'im awake. That's over eighty miles. He called the state land department and had representatives from the state land department come out to talk to 'im on these noises.

Then he said someone was diggin' tunnels, burrowin' under his trailer. He called Santa Fe Railroad to see if they were runnin' a new machine that was keepin' 'im awake. Said his camper trailer was vibratin' at night from the sounds o' this machine. He got every state, local and tribal agency within a hundred miles to try find what machine was keepin' 'im awake and the nearest machine was miles away. The sound o' this machine that never existed finally drove 'im to move 'cause he couldn't sleep no more with that machine runnin'. Thought they were gonna take 'im away to the funny farm. There was never any such machine. He was gone for a year. He came back but he doesn't hear the noises anymore.

Now he's lookin' for a woman. Hasn't had much luck. Hell, he hasn't had *any* luck. The guy is so hard up he's gone over his hundred-thousand-mile warranty on his right hand.

He's so hard up he had a *poster* of a blow-up doll in his room. He finally bought a real, used blow-up doll. He fur-lined the inside of his bathtub spigot. Every knothole in his fence has a name. Both his bed pillows have a hole in them. He thinks that makes it a threesome.

His back went out trying to perform fellatio on himself. The last time he had any pussy, the neighbors looked for their cat for three weeks. He dresses like Charlie Brown and hangs out in front of Neverland.

In his forties he converted to Catholicism hoping to be an altar boy. His own dog won't turn his back on him. The last piece of ass he had was a donkey at the petting zoo.

CHAPTER THIRTY
Picked the Wrong Line

I'm sittin' here workin' one Saturday night. Got a few people in and a U-Haul van pulls up. Out steps a six-foot-three white boy. Skinny as a rail. Got 'im a cowboy hat on and stuff. He steps out o' that U-Haul truck. Walks in the door. He's wearin' spurs. He's drivin' a U-Haul truck and he's wearin' spurs. Well those who've spent some time ridin' horseback know it's hard to drive wearin' your spurs.

He goes to tellin' the story that he's just won the bull ridin' in Phoenix. Well I'm sorry. There ain't never been a bull ridin' contest won by a six-foot-three white boy. That just don't happen. But he's makin' the brag. I look down and his spurs're shiny, his leathers're new. They've never been in the dirt. They have never even seen the rodeo ground. I listen to him talk for a little. I got a girl workin' for me named Verda in them days.

Verda comes to me and says, "Gary, there's two guys in the girls' bathroom back there."

Only queers and drug dealers go to the bathroom together. So I go back there and I take my keys and I pop the bathroom door open. There they're standin'. And the big guy, the white guy, got 'im a big bag o' dope. A big bag o' marijuana and the Zuni guy's got a little baggie and they're transferin'. They've made their deal. Well I reach in there and I swat that dope in the air and it goes everywhere. The white boy turns to fight. That Zuni boy's feet never touch the ground all the way out the door. He was flyin'. He was gone. He was outta here. The white guy turns to fight and I gather his tall, lengthy ass up, beat him off the wall two or three times and ran with 'im to the door and threw 'im out there by his U-Haul truck.

I told him, "Never bring your sorry ass in here agin."

I went back in and went to sweepin' up the floor. Sweepin' up the dope and flushin' it down the toilet. I took their bags back over and walked by and threw 'em in the trash can.

Two Deputies walked in the door.

I said, "How you guys doin'? I sure could o' used you a few minutes ago."

"Well, that's why we came in, Gary. That guy was our undercover agent. We'd sent 'im in to see if he could sell some dope and you beat 'im up and threw 'im out."

I said, "Well, next time you send one o' your boys in let me know and I won't beat 'im up and throw 'im out."

But they quit sendin' in undercover agents after that. The whole deal was they'd sent 'im in to see if he could sell me some dope and the poor guy lost his dope sample, got beat up and thrown out. So then I had to dig what was left o' their dope out o' the trash can and give it back to 'em. They did that to me two or three times in the early days.

One time I'm sittin here. There's a sixty-five-mile-an-hour sign down there 'bout a quarter mile and they're watchin' me with their binocs. So I get out my binocs and I look down there and there's three cop cars of 'em sittin' down there. I think *the hell with this noise* so I go out and git on the bike.

I roll down there and say, "what're you guys doin'?"

"Well, we're watchin' that guy down there in the parkin' lot. We think he's sellin' dope there."

I said, "Which one?"

"Well, that one in the blue car."

I said, "OK. I'll go buy some from him and you go arrest 'im."

"Oh, no. You can't do that. We're jist watchin' 'im."

"Well what the hell you botherin' my business for? If you wanna arrest him for sellin' dope you jist set here. I'll go buy some from 'im, you come arrest 'im and we're done."

"We can't do that. We're jist observin' now."

I said, "Well fine. If you're gonna arrest somebody, arrest somebody. Other than that jist leave us the hell alone."

I got on my bike and came back. They drove off and left. So that whole story 'bout them watchin' some guy, they were watchin' me. All they were doin' was watchin' me. They made up that story that they were watchin' some guy sellin' dope in the parkin' lot.

I had a black guy from Gallup sellin' dope right outside that window. Sellin' junk and Russ was here So I walked 'round the back and I come out; that's before we had all the fence up and stuff. I come out and walk up to 'im right as he was handin' a Zuni guy a joint. He had his hand out the car window. I jist reached up and grabbed his wrist and bent it over the car. Bent his wrist down and he dropped the joint.

I told him, "You git your sorry ass outta here."

"Well, I'm gonna shoot you. Gimme that pistol there."

He tells the guy with 'im to give 'im the pistol out o' the glove box and the guy reaches over and pops the glove box open. I shuck Baby outta my shoulder holster and I stick it right in his temple.

I stick my forty-five right in his temple and say, "Yeah. Go ahead. Pull that gun out o' there. You can go ahead and pull that gun out o' there, or you can fire up this car and pull outta here and leave. Those are your only two choices right now."

So I walked with 'im with my pistol right at his temple as he backed his car up. I had it in his head hard and he backed up the car and he took off.

A week later they came back to kick my ass. Three of 'em showed up and they come in the door and a big one that was gonna be trouble. Me and him locked up right away. I got 'im rolled out the door and right as I drove 'im out the door he went out backwards and he went down. I stepped back and one o' his buddies hit me in the back o' the head hard. Bang! I dropped to my knees out there and the other two came in. I was fixin' to get beat. Bad.

Then Chelsea showed up. My German shepherd showed up. She went to chewin' on 'em and she's got one by the throat. Got 'im down on the ground and got 'im by the throat.

I tell her, "Jist hold 'im there 'til I'm done. Gimme 'nough time to git to my feet and go ahead and stomp on the other two a little bit."

That shepherd held that one down that had hit me in the back o' the head. She held 'im there 'til I got my wits 'bout me and got the other two subdued and stuff. Then I called the dog off and I kicked 'im in the head a couple o' times and let 'em git back in their vehicle and go away. They drove seventy miles from Gallup to kick my ass and they got beat, bit, stomped and drove off with nothin'.

Chapter Thirty-One
Wind is My Friend

Well I'm in a good mood so we'll start off with our local game warden, who we nicknamed The Wind. The Wind is everywhere. I think 'bout twenty years ago he planted a beeper somewhere inside me and every time I cross the line or pull the trigger, he's right there. This guy's amazin'. He is *everywhere*.

One o' the first deer tags I drew in this country, I jump a big old buck down here on the Zuni River over what I figured was close to the Arizona/New Mexico line. In those days there was no boundary lines, no fence line, no markers. I was jist out in the middle of a big ranch. I'd been chasin' this big buck for 'bout three days. One mornin' it was rainin', snowin' off and on. Heavy. It was the last day o' the season and I was on the buck. I had 'im right in front of me. I actually saw one antler walk 'round the ridge. I see that buck so I leave the truck and I start up that Venedita Wash. I git up there in the Malapi and I hear, way off, a truck comin'. I keep hearin' that truck comin' closer and closer down that valley.

I eased up on down the Malapi below the rim so I wasn't sky lighted, eased up to a spot where I could see my truck. As I peeked over there with my binocs, there's the Wind, the new Park Ranger, parked next to my truck. *Oh Shit. What am I gonna do?*

There was a cedar tree up against some fallen rocks made a little shelter, a little cave. It's rainin' hard now. Alright, I'm gonna git in there for a minute and figure what I'm gonna do. So I kind o' tuck in there outta sight and I'm sittin' here and I hear some rocks fallin' and clump, clump, on the rocks and Wind walks right up in front o' me. Turns 'round and takes his glasses up. He's glassin' the other side o' the canyon. He's lookin' for me. He's got no idea where I'm at and I ain't fifty yards behind 'im.

Well, the rain turned to snow and I looked 'round me and wondered *what the heck am I gonna do up in there.* I eased back and sat there and thought 'bout what was facin' me. He hadn't picked up my tracks, didn't know where I was. So I sit there a long time. There's a tree in front o' him. The rain turned to snow and it's snowin' hard. Faced with havin' 'im right there, I figured I better face the music. Only way outta this deal is face it. Besides, it was kind o' tight sittin' there. So I decide, *alright, I'm gonna git outta here.* I ease on outta that little cave, step out on the rocks. I figured he'll hear me.

Well, he doesn't hear me. I start walkin' towards 'im and he jist keeps glassin' the other rim.

I walk up behind 'im and say, "Howdy."

He smacks 'imself in the face with his binocs. He 'bout blacked both his eyes with those binocs. Almost jumped off that little rock ledge. I mean it shook 'im and I don't know 'im, ya know.

He says, "What awuh you doin?"

I said, "Well, if this is official, I'm huntin' coyotes."

He says, "You awuh deah huntin' aren't you?"

"Noooo. I ain't deer huntin. If this is official I'm huntin' coyotes."

"Well, do you have a deah wicense?"

I said, "Yeah. I've got an Arizona deer license."

"Do you wealwize you awuh in New Mexico?"

I said, "Naw, where's the line?" 'Cause in them days there ain't no line. "Where's the line?"

"Well, once you cwoss them powawh lines you awuh in New Mexico."

"No, I've looked at the map and them power lines drift over the state line. I'm not quite sure where they are. That power line isn't on the state line. It comes off out in here somewhere don't it?"

He said, "Well, I know you awuh in New Mexico."

So I walk on to my truck with my rifle in my hand. He's walkin' 'long with me.

He said, "Well, can I see your wifle? I need to ask you for your wifle theyawh."

"Can I see your pistol? I need to ask you for your pistol. If you wanna hold my rifle, I wanna hold your pistol."

"Well, I need to have the numbahs off that wifle for my weport."

"I can tell you what that rifle is. It's a 1939 Savage 250-3000. You don't need any numbers off my rifle."

"Well, I need to give you a ticket."

I said, "If I'm in New Mexico, I'm not takin' a ticket from an Arizona Game Warden."

I git to the truck and put my rifle in the truck.

He says, "I need to know what that wifle is."

I said, "It's a 1939, 250-3000 Savage."

"Well I need the numbahs off it."

"No you don't."

So I git in the truck, fire it up. I drive off and leave him standin' there. He writes a three page letter to the New Mexican Game and Fish that I'm huntin' deer in New Mexico with an Arizona tag.

Now, three months later, in February, I'm sittin' in the bar. In through the door comes double-o-seven, Officer Roger Moore, a New Mexican Game and Fish.

The New Mexico game warden comes in here and says, "Are you Gary Hicks?"

"Yeah"

Sittin' down in the bar here he said, "Well, I need to write cha a ticket."

"For what?"

"For huntin' deer in New Mexico with an Arizona license."

He says, "I got this three page letter from the "Wind" in Arizona explainin' that he witnessed you huntin' deer in New Mexico with an Arizona tag."

I said, 'Yeah, I talked to Wind down there. I was huntin' coyotes, ya know. I worked on that ranch. That was the Hickson ranch. I've enjoyed it for years. I pushed a lot o' cows there. I almost died there. So I was kind of at home. I'll tell you this. If I wouldn't take a ticket from an Arizona Game Warden in New Mexico, I'm damn sure not takin' a ticket from a New Mexico Game Warden sittin' in a bar in Arizona. I suggest you just git on outta here."

He wrote out a warnin', threw it on the bar and walked out. Off he went and I never git a ticket off either one of 'em.

Wind and I, we gained a mutual respect for each other after that. Since then Wind and I have grown close. We've become friends, mostly 'cause he does an excellent job.

There are some good stories 'bout 'im. When he first come to this country, he took an old cowboy named Bill Mann out to witness for some guys that poached a deer.

Bill walked up there with the Wind and Wind said, "Yayuh. They killed that deah wight heah. You see that hayuh?"

Bill said, "Yeah. I see the hair but they didn't kill a deer."

"Yayuh. The hayuh's wite heah."

"Yeah, but that's antelope hair."

So Wind, comin' out here from Oklahoma, learned a little 'bout our country.

One time my daughter and I and 'nother guy were fixin' fence on the south end o' the ranch. If you've ever fixed fence, it ain't a lot o' fun. You've got a bag and a hammer and tools and some wire and some staples and you go from post to post down the fence. Well there's three of us leap froggin' down the line. All of a sudden, through the trees, I see the Wind's truck. He parks down the road about three hundred yards out there, gits, outta his truck and starts walkin' to us. We keep goin' down the fence line and I'm hammerin' staples.

He walks up, "What cha all doin?"

I said, "I'm huntin' deer with a claw hammer. What do ya think I'm doin?"

"Oh no, no, no, I didn't wealwise this was youah fence line. I thought this was somebody else's fence line."

"Well if its somebody else's fence line I wouldn't be fixin it would I."

Over the years we've had some funny ones. After I had some surgery a while back I run into him at Wilbur's grocery story.

I went up to 'im and said, "Hey, Wind, while I got cha here I got thirty-six staples in my stomach right now. I jist wanted you to check that beeper. They might o' pulled it outta me when they operated on me and you may need to re-install it."

What I figure is, 'bout the beeper, somewhere in the past twenty years, he snuck somethin' into my food or somehow he installed a beeper somewhere up my ass. When my truck crosses the bound'ry line that beeper goes off. If there's a coyote in my pasture near my calf and I pull out my twenty-two mag that beeper goes off. Now whether he's got a camera on his cell so he can see what I'm actually seein', I don't know.

Sometimes he shows up, sometimes he doesn't show up. So I figure if he doesn't show up, I'm in the right. 'Cause the Wind is everywhere. If I pull the trigger, he's there. If I cross the line he's there. That's what he's good at. When he shows up I've done somethin' wrong. When he shows up I'm right on the edge o' bein' on the edge. When he doesn't show up, I figure I'm doin' OK.

Wind's a good one. I hear stories 'bout him. Everybody in the country talks about 'im. He's famous. I don't care where you're at, what you're doin', what time o' day or night it is, the Wind blows in. I mean he's everywhere, and I respect 'im for it. He has my utmost respect. Now he's bin warden twenty-three years. Maybe, gittin' up close to retirein'. Don't know who we'll git to replace 'im. If he does half the job the Wind does, he'll do just fine.

Chapter Thirty-Two
Stranded and Stupid

Stranded and stupid. When people ask why I'm out here in the middle o' nowhere I tell 'em, "No, middle o' nowhere is six miles west."

Ahh, but we are darn sure remote. We are remote to the fact that we have no power lines. We have no services. On a call o' 'shots fired, I need help', it was forty-seven minutes before help got here. You can empty a lot o' clips in forty-seven minutes. Fire protection is me and a shovel. I've put out more brush fires 'round here than I remember. All kinds o' fires. Lightnin', man caused, human car wrecks. So we are remote.

Every now and then I get stranded people. Get lots. Some of 'em just dummer than a box o' rocks. Some of 'em genuinely accidental.

Had a guy pull 'round the corner one time. Had a seventy-four Chevy Vega. Pulls up. White smoke is billowin' outta this Vega when he comes 'round the corner. He's got a blown head gasket. I know for sure o' that. Motor's dumpin' water. And he pulls in. Tall guy maybe six foot five, real slender. Gits outta the Vega looks 'round a little, opens the hood, looks in. Well, I wait 'im out. I wait a couple o' hours with him walkin' 'round lookin' at that vehicle before I go out. Figure things are usually not my business 'till I'm drug into 'em.

So I go out, "You're gonna need a wrecker."

He says, "Come from nine kids in the family."

"You got a blown head gasket. You got water in your oil."

He said, "I like peanut butter and jelly."

I never got an answer out of 'im. This went on all day. That night I took him a peanut butter and jelly sandwich and a gallon o' water. I left 'im out there. A guy don't sleep real well on them nights. In the mornin' I git up. Durin' the night he had gotten the engine outta that little Chevy Vega all by 'imself. Had it sittin' on top o' the roof. I still never git an answer outta him.

If I would ask him, "Uh, Bud, you got family or anything?"

He'd say, "They told me I was talkin' okay when they let me out."

That and peanut butter and jelly were the only two things I got outta him in two days. All of a sudden here comes the sheriff's rig. Comes whippin' up to the window, they need a pint bottle o' Lord Calvert. Three of 'em in there.

So I tell 'em, "Guys, uh, I need some help. I got problems here. This guy's in another world. He ain't all here. He can't rebuild that engine out here. I can't communicate with 'im so I can't help 'im."

They whipped that blazer over there in front o' that little Vega, hook a chain on it and drag 'im two miles down the road. And cut 'im loose! *And cut him loose!* When they came back through they *told* me they'd done that. I wasn't real happy with 'em so I got 'nother couple peanut butter and jelly sandwiches together and 'nother gallon o' water and I went down there. He was gone. I never saw 'im agin. His car sat there a long time. Over a week. I was surprise it stayed there that long. Somebody hauled it and then it was gone.

I get people stranded here who're just flat arrogant. You *are goin' to help me right now and I do not owe you a dime for it.* They talk that way and I'm the only help they've got in miles. Stranded and stupid is what I call it.

One Sunday night after we'd closed up and I'd gone to bed, a bunch o' friends had an all-night party down here under the trees. Well it was that cool time o' year and they'd run the heaters quite a bit and they were outta gas.

When I come 'round in the mornin' it was early. It'd be about seven o-clock Monday morning, my uncle was here. He was out here cleanin' up and I was in back sortin' money.

My uncle come back and said, "Gary, there's a guy here. They say they're outta gas."

Well at this time I didn't know my bouncer, Ervin., was with 'em. I walked out and here was a guy layin' on the bar. Layin' all the way 'cross here. He's got one hand balancin' himself and he's got ahold o' this pint. He's stealin' a pint o' cheap vodka off my back shelf and he's laid out all the way 'cross the bar. So I jist step up and drive 'im in a pile right there. He's all laid out there in mid-air and I just drive 'im to the ground. I gather 'im up and git 'im on out the door where everybody's waitin' for 'im.

I tell 'im, "You stupid son-of-a-bitch. Here I'm walkin' out here to git gas for you. I'm tryin to help you and you're stealin' from me."

But I went ahead and got 'im five gallons o' gas 'cause my bouncer was with 'im and stuff. They took off down the road and they were all mad at 'im. They loaded 'im up in that wagon and they took 'im down the road there at the top-o-the-world. They stopped and educated 'im 'bout how stupid he was. Left 'im there in a pile like Wily Coyote and drove off. Stupid and stranded, they don't go well together.

Chapter Thirty-Three
Dealin' with White Folks

When I first got here the hired help that was here, one of 'em robbed me and run off. 'Bout twenty-five hundred dollars disappeared along with 'im. Then there was a couple shysters runnin' this place and I'd run them off, too. There were battles over that.

Then I hired an old girl livin' out here in the trees. Bonnie. Bonnie was livin' out here in the trees with her husband and I think three little kids, or two and one on the way, yeah that was it. They was sawin' wood for a livin'. They'd been livin' out there in the trees for 'bout a year. I drove down there to town and got directions 'bout how to find 'em out here. When I drove up there, the husband come walkin' out of a big cedar tree. I noticed there was some tissue paper 'round. I went ahead and hired her. As I drove out, I looked at that tree that he'd come walkin' out of. I realized there wasn't no outhouse anywhere out there. I looked and that tree had a big forked limb 'bout two foot off the ground. One fork raised up high off the ground kind o' like a back rest and the other was smooth and round. They were jist crappin' in the fork o' that tree and it was piled out in the open underneath there. Now they lived out there almost two years and never built an outhouse. Just crapped in the fork o' that tree. The whole family.

Her job ended when I'd gone to Phoenix to git my liquor license. I was fightin' liquor control. I come back walkin' in here 'bout four o'clock in the afternoon. It was a hot summer day. Door's wide open.

I say, "Hello the house," and I git no answer.

I looked 'round, checked the bathrooms and the walk-in cooler and there ain't nobody there. Cash register, I pop it open. There's money in it. Close it. Walk 'round and open up the door to the office. My barmaids' husband's layin' there on the floor. Passed out cold with a tipped over rocket o' cheap vodka and a sub machine gun. Locked and loaded. But the door was wide open in the middle o' the day. I locked up and hauled his sorry butt out there. He'd beat her up. Got drunk and beat her up and run her off and took control o' the bar. Doin' me a favor. Some favors guys do for you aren't favors. I called the law on that deal. He went off to jail. So she comes back. When he got outta jail she worked for me 'nother couple o' months and then they packed up 'n went to the valley or somethin'. He wound up goin' to prison down there.

Over the years, the forty-acre maggots that I've hired over here, only one, Johnnie, ever worked out. Only one out o' all these people that live out here in the trees, who are hidin' from society, they don't make the greatest employees. Son-of-a-gun, can't figure that one out.

Years ago, I got quoted in the newspaper sayin' the only white folks that lived out here were either runnin' from the law or couldn't fit in anywhere else. I don't know if it's changed all that much. I won't call anybody neighbor 'til they've lived here over a year. Now-a-days, with computers and the new money . . . there's lots o' new money out there. People are comin' out and stayin'. And maybe I need to change my ways. Not be tellin' 'em the truth. Not tell 'em that water may not be in existence. Not tellin' 'em if it exists, it's not economically feasible when you gotta spend thirty-thousand dollars for water.

Now-a-days, these idiots are payin' up to five hundred dollars an acre for forty acres. This is blow sand. This is high desert. They spend fifteen- to twenty-thousand for forty acres and when they realize that water is thirty-thousand and a fence 'round it is eight or nine thousand and this is open range country and cows come and go where they want, some of 'em give up.

Then, back in the days when it got cold, uh, and it did agin this year, them twenty below winters run 'em out o' here, eleven, seventeen, eighteen below. I've seen eighteen inches o' snow overnight. And these people come out o' California and they come out o' the big cities back east unprepared for this kind o' life.

Chapter Thirty-Four
Help's Help

Ahh, I've had a bunch o' crazy bar maids. Bonnie that was livin' out there in the trees was the first of 'em. Sue and Dixie, a couple o' lesbian girls, still have my utmost respect.

They caused quite a stir 'cause at one point I was livin' out here with three women and in our red-neck, Christian county they became the talk o' the town. What other peoples' sexual choices are their business not mine. But, uh, Sue and Dixie lived here a long time 'bout a year I guess, maybe longer.

The last time I saw Sue, I was sittin' in a bar in Rock Ridge. She'd seen my truck out front so she come whippin' in. She was on some sort o' crystal meth or somethin'. She'd been campin' two or three days out in the trees. She come walkin' in that bar. Her normally curly hair was wild lookin' anyway but she's got that three-days campin' hair. Kinky, wild, huge three-day campin' trip hair. All crystal methed up.

She come walkin' in the door and yells at me. "Hey boss."

I turned 'round and looked at her and I said, "Sue, you look like an exploded cockle burr."

She loved my jokes. One time I told her, "Sue, ya know, if you ever had sex with a man your hymen would break and your balls would drop."

She told everybody she knew. She thought that was one o' the funniest jokes she'd ever heard. Yeah.

But they were good help. Saved a lot o' time and were lots o' laughs. Like all good things they come to an end.

I had another Susan workin' for me. She was one o' these forty acre maggots out here. Lived in a pickup camper. I'd lost some help, I don't remember what for. So I hired the old girl. She come in and had worked 'bout three weeks. I thought she was a little different but I didn't have any complaints. She cleaned up the place. She was workin' one day. I was busy. We had a delivery goin' on. I had a bunch o' people at once and I was busy. She was workin'. I walked by right after the delivery and there was three bottles o' liquor sittin' on the counter. As I walked by talkin' to another gentleman I picked 'em up and set 'em up on the shelf so she wouldn't have to reach 'em. Then I walked on in the back room. Oh, I remember. That day my dog had got run over. Not Chelsea, Saydro got run over that day so I was not in a real good mood anyway. So as I walked by, I put them bottles on the shelf and I walked on in the back room.

All of a sudden she was hot on my heels and she said, "I jist can't work like this."

I turned 'round and said, "What?"

She says, "I jist can't work like this. Now I have to crawl up there and git them bottles back down and dust 'em 'cause I hadn't dusted 'em yet. You're makin' my job twice as hard as it needs to be. I can't put up with this."

I turned around and said, "Git your ass out the door. I'm done with you."

She cussed me all the way out the door. Never came back in. I gave her twenty dollars or whatever I owed her ya know. I owed her for maybe one day or so. I kicked her out o' the place. Well she filed for unemployment on me from the looney bin in Iowa. 'Bout two months later we got a note that she was in the looney bin in Iowa and she was tryin' to file for unemployment. That's the last I ever saw, or heard o' Forty-Acre Susan. I was glad she was gone.

Chapter Thirty-Five
Miss Communication

That people do different things, I've always been a kind o' student o' human behavior. I'm a good judge o' character. Not perfect, but I spend a lot o' time figurin' out why people do things. What they're doin'. Why they're doin' it. I'm the kind o' guy that likes to sit back and watch and figure it out before I do anything. Ah, uh, some people I never figured out. If I can't, I don't think anybody can.

I've never been a tough man. I've always been a little too tender. I've never been a violent man, but I've never run from a fight. I prefer to run at 'em 'stead o' runnin' from 'em. I have a nervous reaction and one o' the bar maids commented on it. When a man is in my face and it's gonna come to violence I have a nervous twitch and I put my hands behind my back. I'll stand face to face with the gentleman and give 'im the first shot by puttin' my hands behind my back. Elaine used to say if she saw me put my hands behind my back she knew the fight was imminent. It was gonna happen. I'm gittin' too old for this. I don't fight anymore. I'm not afraid of 'em. I'll fight if forced, but I don't do it for fun anymore.

One time Russ was workin' the door and that Sunday we're busy. I'm workin' the drive up window.

Russ says, "Hey Gary. There's some guys stealin' wood out the back."

So I told 'im, "Jist watch 'em. I'll go 'round back and you start up there in a minute."

He waited a second and I headed up out the back and when I get up there, there's one guy on my wood pile and he's throwin' wood over the fence to 'nother guy. The other guy, he's stackin' it 'cause they don't even have a truck. They're gonna use the wood to buy 'em a ride home. So they're stackin' it out by the edge o' the road.

I git up there and I yell at the guy, "Hey!"

He's up on the wood pile so he tries to jump over the fence. When he does the firewood moves underneath his feet and he winds up goin' sideways over the fence. When we walk 'round the fence he's hangin' upside down with his foot wedged between the board slats. Got 'imself trapped. Hung there. Russ and I go to pick 'im up and we git 'im up and we're holdin' 'im up in the air. Now the fence is all of 'bout six and a half foot up there. So we got 'im up over our heads and we're holdin' 'im. I gotta take one hand loose and knock his foot outta the fence 'cause it's jammed in there. After 'bout the third hit, I knocked his foot out o' the wedge o' the fence and I step back. Well Russ stepped back too. The guy lands in a pile from six and a half feet in the air between our feet.

I say to Russ, "I thought you had 'im."

Russ says, "I thought you had 'im."

Fact was, neither one of us had 'im. Then we make the poor guy git up and haul all o' the wood back over the fence. It was funny and nobody got beat up. I've been real lucky at Witch Well. I've had to fight a little but I haven't lost. I can't afford to lose. It's not an option . . . not an option. This thing is vicious. It's now and it's over and that's all there is to it. There's no such thing as a fair fight unless I win. I've fought multiple assailants on multiple occasions. That's never fun.

Chapter Thirty-Six
Hillbillies

Hillbillies. Texas hillbillies. They show up outta Phoenix. I git so tired of 'em showin' up here every mornin' wantin' to sell me a chain saw, twenty-two rifle, whatever. Tryin' to sell me whatever they can sell to git booze. Momma's toothless with a wad o' chew in her mouth. I'm sure she wakes up with it there. Stained, filthy people. There's two boys, momma, and a dad.

I tell those boys, "Why don't you guys keep showin' up here every mornin' at seven o'clock so I can kick your goddam asses and git regular exercise? 'Cause I'm sick and tired o' seein' you every mornin'. If you start showin' up here at seven I'll jist kick your ass instead o' exercisin'. That'll make me feel better." Well they got the point a little bit.

They git in a fight out at the house one night. They're all drinkin' half gallons o' vodka. Don't know where they got it. I don't even sell half gallons o' vodka. Never have. But the whole family's in there drinkin' vodka. 'Bout two in the mornin', one-thirty, maybe, I'd jist gone to bed. Bang, Bang on the window. Debbie gits out here before I do. There's Momma covered in blood standin' at the window at two o'clock in the mornin'.

I git out here and she says, "Call the law. I jist killed my boy."

So I called the law, she takes off. Sheriff's department shows up. Their boy ain't dead, yet. He's sittin' at the kitchen table. They're *all* sittin' there. All four of 'em drinkin' from half gallons o' cheap vodka.

Sheriff's department walks in the door. Boy's gut-shot point blank with a twenty gauge shotgun. Got a hole blown through him. He's sittin' there pourin' vodka outta it. Pourin' it down his throat. He's 'bout twenty-seven years old.

Cops say, "What's goin' on here?"

Momma says, "I shot the son-of-a-bitch."

Daddy says, "No, I shot this son-of-a-bitch."

Brother says, "No, I shot the son-of-a-bitch."

Boy says, "No, I shot myself."

They're all lyin'. They finally air lift him to Phoenix. Now, it takes that sorry little bastard ten days to die. He gits gut-shot with bird shot and he was sittin' there drinkin' for several hours after he was gut-shot and they fly 'im all the way to Phoenix. Takes this tough little bastard ten days to die.

Our sheriff's department never pinned a charge on anyone in the room. He was murdered by his own family. And no one was ever charged. They couldn't know who to charge. Couldn't charge anybody. All they could prove was he did not shoot 'imself 'cause he couldn't reach the trigger and make the wound that was made 'cause he was shot from about ten feet away. Shadow of a doubt. Couldn't charge any o' the three 'cause each was sayin' they'd shot him

To this day that family o' hillbillies still cuss me, that I'm a no good bastard 'cause I won't let 'em in here. I won't. The last time I threw 'em outta here I was serious. The boy called me a name.

I walked out to the bar and he said, "There's that sorry, fuckin', asshole."

Well I'm not gonna take that from anybody in my bar unless that's someone I've bled and lived with. Someone's in my heart he can get away with that, but if you're a strange hillbilly from out in the trees you ain't got chance one o' gittin' away with that. They still live out here, but they're not allowed in Witch Well Tavern.

CHAPTER THIRTY-SEVEN
Family Affair

I gotta fight goin' on outside that window one day. I storm out there to break it up and I walked out there and one o' the Bosen boys has got another guy's head up against the wall. And he's just drillin' 'im with his right hand.

I step up there and I grab 'im by the shoulder and pull 'im off and say, "What the hell do you think you're doin?"

He says, "Oh, its ok Gary. It's ok. He's my brother."

Now here he is pastin' his head to the wall with a right hand. I didn't realize it was alright, 'cause it's a family problem. Family affair.

Back in those days we were always havin' trouble with them Bosen boys. They used to like to come out 'n fight. Drinkin', fightin' . . . that was their claim to fame. They were out here lookin' for a fight, harassin' customers one day. There were three of 'em. So I went out there and when I was chewin' on 'em, the little one throws a quart bottle at me and charges. When he throws that quart I duck. When he misses me with that quart, I stand up right when he gits to me, I hit him hard. He dropped. Bomb! Down he goes. Then I made a little error. I figured he was done.

I locked up with the big one and he and I were tradin' blows. That little one had come 'round. He crawled on the ground and got a hold o' my feet after I'd written him off. He was tryin' to pull me down so I reached up and grabbed the big one in the eye sockets on my way down and drug 'im down with me. So I was tryin' to let go of one and grind his face in the gravel and keep a hold o' the other by the eye sockets. Then the third one come in and he started kickin' me in the middle. I'm startin' to lose. I'm startin' to lose.

Well Clifton Bowannie showed up like a freight train. He dove into the middle o' the pile and that knocked two of 'em over. I finished off the little one. I went ahead and ground his face into the gravel, got up and stomped on the back o' his neck so he stayed there. While Clifton was holdin' the third one down, now I've got a hold o' the big one. We tore the gate off the fence by the bathroom right there. Yeah, there used to be a gate there.

I looked over at Clifton and I said, "You jist hold 'im there. I'm gonna break this one's nose."

I rolled that Bastard over and I said, 'You ready?"

He looks up at me and BOOM, I broke his nose.

Bloods runnin' everywhere. I said, "You want me to break anything else?"

I told Clifton, "OK, just hold that one and I'll come break his nose, too."

So he held 'im for a while and I went over and broke his nose, too. That was the last day I had to mess with the Bosen boys. They went off to find 'nother place to fight after that. Without Clifton's help they'd 'o got my ass 'cause I made a mistake and wrote that little one off. 'Cause when I hit 'im, ya know, the lights went out and down he went. He jist didn't stay down.

Chapter Thirty-Eight
False Bravado

Here's one for the books. We got a guy down in the village. One Friday-the-thirteenth a couple years ago he comes back from fightin' fires. Lots o' firefighters in the village. He's all horned up. Couldn't find a woman. Well one thing leads to another which leads to hell. There it was, Friday, April thirteenth, late eighties, early nineties. Well I'd rented a truck. The EPA had ordered all the stations to have tests done on their underground fuel tanks 'n if you weren't gonna continue to use 'em you had to pull 'em outta the ground. So I rented some equipment and I had a couple guys workin' here. Workin' on pullin' some underground fuel tanks. I was at the top o' the hill unloadin' sacks o' concrete outta the truck.

A little grey car with dark windows and a Jeep Cherokee come barrelin' over the hill chasin' each other. They went to playin' bumper pool in the parkin' lot. Bangin' off each other. I started walkin' down the hill. They drove up next to me. When I walked 'round the front o' the truck they drove up next to me.

The guy in the passenger side o' the Cherokee yelled, "Help me Gary. He's gonna git me."

Then the guy jumped out o' his little grey car and started toward the Cherokee. The Cherokee took off and went down the hill. The guy got back in his car and headed back after 'em so I walked down the hill to the front o' the bar.

When I got there Barney jumped out 'n he was yellin' at me, "Help me Gary, he's gonna git me."

Knife Wing gits outta the little grey car and he's yellin' threats and stuff at Barney. I don't know what's goin' on. I don't realize Barney's with Knife Wing's wife. The guy's gonna cut Barney.'s head off and stuff and I git in between 'em.

I tell Knife Wing., "Git the hell outta here," and whatever else and tell Barney, "Git inside the door." He gits in.

Then Knife Wing starts threatenin' me, "I'm gonna kill you. I'm gonna come back in the middle o' the night 'n burn you down."

He had a gun in his hand. He was leavin'. I had one in mine. As he started to git in his car, he turned and repeated the threat that he was gonna come back and burn me down. So I put one behind his feet.

Told 'im, "Git outta here or I'll tear your head off with the next one. Git the hell off my property.

So he got in his little car and drove 'round the side o' the gravel truck and a lowboy we had parked in the front o' the parkin' lot. When he come out o' the other side o' the gravel truck he had his window down. Had a nine millimeter out the window pointed at me and he emptied it. As he was emptyin' it on me, I rolled and dropped to my knee, then I rolled up next to the truck and sought refuge. He kept hammerin' away and I realized he was drivin' 'round the lowboy and he was gonna git the angle on me. So I rolled out into the parkin' lot, come up on one knee and I started returnin' fire. Never had any practice shootin' at a guy drivin' by hammerin' at me out a window. You can actually see the lead in the air. Things slow down. Gravel spittin' 'round me. Bullets slammin' into the truck and stuff, blowin' tires. We're alive and dead at the same time.

I run outta ammo and so did he. He charges up the hill in his car. He jack-knifes his car. I don't know he has two pieces. I figure he's reloadin'. I come towards the window. Debbie's standin' there with a box o' shells and another pistol and she's reloadin'. I hand her the clip and she goes to loadin'.

Then I yell, "Everybody git inside. Everybody git outta here."

Everybody gits inside the bar and I said "Now git me that riot shotgun."

Debbie, by then, had reloaded mine so I came up towards the door and he saw me comin' from the top o' the hill where he was jack-knifed and he gave up and spun on out o' here.

This guy claims to be a bunch o' things. I didn't know he was New Mexico Tri-County Drug Enforcement. I didn't know he was DEA. I didn't know he was a certified witness for the FBI. He went to Zuni and turned in a five shot thirty-eight boot gun. Filed charges against me. Well there were nine millimeter slugs all over this place. He's hammerin' at me with a nine and he got there and turned in a little five shot thirty-eight. That's when I figured out he had two guns.

Cost me thousands o' dollars but it cost me far more emotionally. Scars a man still carries and will carry. They ordered me not to have a gun for a year.

So I asked 'em, "Well, where you gonna keep 'em?"

They said, "Bring your guns in and we'll store 'em here."

"Store 'em where?"

"We got some lockers down in the basement in the old jail."

I said, "How many lockers you got?"

They said, "How many guns you got?"

"Quite a few."

"Well give us a list."

So I comprised a list for 'em 'cause I was required to do so by law. I gave 'em a list o' seventy-seven different firearms. Had to rent a storage unit and store 'em for one year. They wanted 'em all, but I s'pose if a guy gave 'em a list o' seventy-seven he'd missed maybe three or four. But it was an up-against-the-wall deal. The FBI came and testified on his behalf. The state charged 'im. I was convicted of a misdemeanor for an unlawful discharge of a fire arm. It was a big downside in this whole thing.

This is the funniest part 'bout it. We go to the judge. When the judge says we can't have a fire arm for a year, my wife held all the money in those days.

My wife says, "Well there ain't no way I'm gonna haul this kind o' money every week without a way to protect myself."

So the judge said, "Well, Debbie, you jist keep your pistol in your purse so he doesn't have access to it."

Debbie looks at me and says, "Don't pick up my purse."

My probation officer kept the gun that I used in the crime, for me in his house for a year so it never got destroyed. Then I got it back. It's called

Baby, my high-dollar, custom-floated forty-five. Nice little gun. Baby's been around. Baby's real loud. When Baby talks everybody listens.

Here's how everything comes back to bite ya. What I didn't know durin' this whole deal until days later, ten days later, before they came and arrested me was that Ivan had two kids in the car. Oh, yeah, he chased people thirty miles with his kids in the car. He was on a high-speed chase for thirty miles with two children in it. So they charged me with endangerin' a child. I didn't even know they were there in that little dark-windowed, New Mexico car. And it was an undercover car he was drivin' and he was chasin' his wife and 'nother man while heavily armed with two children in his car. He walked and it cost me tens o' thousands o' dollars.

The county attorney told me, "Either you plead guilty of a misdemeanor or we're gonna charge you with a felony. We'll close you down. We'll take your liquor license. It'll all be over."

I told him, "Do what you gotta do. Jist tell me where I sign." Yeah that deal was interestin'.

I've had some good Friday-the-thirteenths, too. I killed a trophy, muzzle-loader mule deer on a Friday-the-thirteenth. I killed an archery bull elk on Friday-the-thirteenth. Yeah. I've had some good Friday-the-thirteenths. I got nothin' 'gainst 'em. But that one will always stick in my mind.

Chapter Thirty-Nine
Spectation

One day we got cars out front here. Parkin' lot's busy and there's a guy and a girl out there and another car pulls up next to 'em. Well it's his wife and she's caught 'im with that other girl. She gits 'round there and she's chewin' on 'im and pretty soon the fight's 'bout to start. Me and my help are workin'. I guess we got 'bout four of us workin 'that day and she goes to pullin' him outta that car and she can't git 'im outta the car. She's beatin' the snot outta this guy. And he's doin' everything he can to stay in that car. And she is punchin', kickin', scratchin' she's jist beatin' the holy shit outta him. But she can't git 'im outta the car, ya know.

The girl with 'im, she jumps and runs and gits in 'nother truck and takes off. So I git 'round here and I make up score cards and when she finally gits tired o' beatin' 'im up she stands up. All four of us help, we stand up at the window and we flash up score cards 5.2, 5.4, 5.5. I gave her a 3.9. She kicked his ass superbly but never got 'im outta that car. If she'd a got him outta that car it'd been a perfect 6 ya know, but she couldn't. When we flashed up our cards out in the parkin' lot, lord ya know the party rolled on.

One day Debbie's workin' behind the bar. She'd only been here maybe a month and had never been around Native Americans much in her life. It's a Sunday and we're busy as hell.

We had a couple Zuni girls sittin' at the bar and they were aggravated, speakin' in their native tongue. Another Zuni lady came in madder'n hell.

She comes up to one of 'em and they are rattlin'. They're goin' after each other in their native tongue just la-te-da. An altercation was imminent.

Debbie stood there between the ladies not knowin' a single word o' what they were sayin' or knowin' what the fight was all 'bout.

Debbie's standin' there kind o' wide-eyed.

She kept sayin', "Ladies, ladies, we don't need this."

All of a sudden outta this Zuni woman's mouth comes, *you gave my husband penis infection.*" Those were the only words of English that came outta her. Debbie instantly knew what the fight was 'bout.

Debbie threw her hands up in the air and said, "OK, she's yours. I got no part of this. I'm outta this. I say you kick her ass."

Chapter Forty
Smelled That Comin'

Let's do a little on Ernistine Murphy. She moved into this country quite a while back. One o' the forty-acre maggots out in the trees. The first time we meet her; she's up there tellin' my wife she's gonna build a post office 'cross the road.

Well, my wife says, "No, we've already checked into the mail delivery and they won't deliver mail out here."

"Oh no, I'm gonna build a post office right across the road."

My wife tells her, "Prob'ly not on account 'o that's our property 'cross the road."

Well, then she was gonna force my wife to give up that property to build a post office. Right of Eminent Domain, whatever. That was the first I ever heard o' her. Then in the process o' puttin' together my cattle operation I'd written letters to neighborin' property owners 'bout access o' my cattle on open range.

Ernistine had got hold o' one o' them letters. And she tried to blow it all outta proportion that I was runnin' the law out here. She wrote a letter to the editor o' the newspaper. Said I was runnin' the sheriff's department out o' the Witch Well Bar. I still got the clippin' from the newspaper. Wrote a big letter. Said I was runnin' cattle, trespassin' on everybody's land and the Sheriff's department wouldn't mess with me 'cause I had the sheriff's department in my pocket. Said some o' my cattle ate her tulips. What the hell. I don't know nothin' 'bout no tulips.

I heard all this stuff she said 'bout me and I went down and talked to her and tried to straighten her out that I wasn't runnin' cattle anywhere near her property. Didn't have anything to do with her. Wasn't any o' her business. She don't know what she's talkin' 'bout, open range 'n stuff. Then she comes up here and I told her to leave me alone.

She said, "We're gonna live here whether you like it or not.

I jist said, "We'll see."

What I meant by that was these people come and go out here in these trees. We never call one of 'em a neighbor till he's been here over a year. Then we gotta see how he acts. What he's growin' or manufacturin'. So I jist meant we'll see if she lives there very long or not. Well the old girl hated me for a couple o' years and then just out o' pure meanness, she up and died.

This is my definition o' pure meanness. I traveled back and forth to Phoenix a little in the old days and there was a Whiting gas station right when you came into Show Low, Arizona from the north. It had the filthiest outhouse I'd ever been in, in my life. It was an actual restroom in the buildin' but I've been in cleaner outhouses. I hated to even use it. Ernistine's husband hated her so bad that when she died, he had her cremated and he flushed her down that toilet in Show Low.

Yeah, even though he hated her so much, they were still married when she died. He's had three wives that I know of and all of 'em are dead.

Charley Bernstine lived out there not too far from 'em. Charley was a good old man. Had a couple quarter horses he should o' fenced in but he never did. Nobody'd heard from 'im for a little while. He had family back in Illinois. They'd got hold o' the sheriff's department to see if they could raise an answer from 'im. They come out here and I was goofin' off that day. They wanted to know if I knew where he lived.

I knew where his trailer was out there so I got in with em' and we went out there to see if we could raise old Charley from his trailer. See if he's out there. When we pulled up his truck was there. We figured he was 'round somewhere. Went up to that trailer door and the sheriff knocked and called on and called on 'im. No answer, no answer, I stepped up there next to Ike. He opened that door and we knew where Charley was. The smell in that trailer house from that dead man layin' in there for over a week was unbelievable. Now it ain't his job to confirm Old Charley, so

I had to go in there and confirm. I wanted no part o' that confirmation. But, uh, Yeah, Charley had two or three horses out there with 'im, he'd come from the east Ohio or Illinois. Somethin like that. Settled down out here. Don't know what happened to those horses.

Chapter Forty-One
History Denied

The greatest hunt I've ever been on was with my huntin' partner, Chino. He drew a muzzle-loader elk tag for a hunt over in Zuni. I didn't have one. We'd helped each other before so Chino asked if I'd help 'im. We were chasin' a bull we called Roberto. Roberto lived up in the corner o' the reservation.

He was a big, impressive bull livin' in some o' the thickest scrub-brush country you could ever find. Real bushy country. Real thick, heavy country. Hard to walk ten feet without havin' to turn. In that blow-sand country, tracks were the only thing you had to go by.

Then one day we hit things jist right. We'd picked up his tracks in the sand that mornin'. We'd had rain the night before and we picked up tracks o' him and his cows goin' up into some real thick cedar country to bed down. We had fresh tracks so we went after the herd and we Osama'd up on 'em ya know. There wasn't a lot o' visibility and darned if we didn't bump right into 'em.

That big old bull jumps up, stands sideways, and he's four hundred inches o' horn. He's huge. My partner fires from thirty five yards broadside, KABOOM. *Misses 'im.*

Well, that broke up the herd and the big bull went over the fence. Jumped out o' the unit. So we turned 'round and called it a day, a little disgusted with ourselves.

You hunt elk mainly in the mornin' and in the evenin' so we come back in the afternoon. It's late September. It's perfect elk huntin' and this thunder cloud is movin' in. It breaks up the herd. We chase after the bull on foot for a ways. It's jist a total bust. Now we're disgusted. We're mad at ourselves and all of our stupidity. But we know that bull is gonna wanna gather his cows back up.

We knew where there's a clearin' back hidden in the trees so we head for it. When we git to that clearin' we can hear Roberto buglin'. He's come over the ridge. He's comin' back into our unit to gather his cows up. We can hear four or five different bulls buglin' in the valley.

We'd come into that clearin'. Him and 'nother bull we call Eight Ball, a big eight by eight bull, huge bull, but there is no match to Roberto. They're out there fightin' in the middle o' that clearin' and the thunderstorm moves in. We Osama up through the sage brush there in that clearin'. We git up there and the lightnin' crashes and thunder pops and the wind blows and Chino raises up. Those two bulls stop fightin' and the cows start movin' toward the trees. Roberto is 'bout fifty yards and KABOW Chino fires *and misses again.*

We know with the number of other bulls in the country the fight's gonna be on. Jist before dark, that same night, that bull's gonna come back to git his cows. And he's gonna fight anything that's near any 'o his cows. As luck would have it; 'long 'bout dusk, we moved, goin' towards the clearin' and the bulls start buglin'. They start firin' off challenges and they start to roll and rumble and they're gittin' loud. A thunder storm moves in and we got thunder and lightnin' poppin' and big bull elk all 'round us and they're yellin' and screamin'.

Roberto comes out into the clearin' that we've got to. We move into the trees and here comes Roberto 'round the trees full speed, stops and bugles. Yells at us. Roars. *And Chino misses.* He hands me the rifle and the lightnin' crashes and the bulls go into the trees.

Out comes Eight Ball. Well, the bulls spin 'round and they git to fightin' agin. Eight Ball and Roberto, they're slammin' each other. With the lightnin' and thunder poppin', they don't even know we're there. Them cows 'n calves and young satellite bulls are runnin' in every direction. These two massive bulls are hammerin' each other over the cows. We're in the middle o' thirty or more elk in the middle o' the rut and the fight goes on. And the fight goes on.

All the time we' kind 'o Osama up on 'em. All the time we're tryin to sneak up on 'em. As they move toward them trees they break to fight.

We got 'em at forty yards walkin' right by us in unison. *And my partner misses 'im agin.*

The thunder and lightnin' crashes 'n the bulls yell. Eight Ball runs 'round and they go to fightin' agin. We're standin' there tryin' to re-load that muzzle loader. And the rain starts comin' and the lightnin' pops and the bulls fight . . . and the bulls fight. We git reloaded; move on into the trees with 'em a little. They're feelin' uncomfortable but they're busy. They move into the trees and we move in with 'em. Out Roberto comes agin and KAWACK. My partner *shoots a tree ten feet from him.* He's so busy lookin' at them horns he can't even look down that rifle.

By now I'm gittin' frustrated as hell.

He yells at me, "You jist shoot him. You shoot him."

"No. Let's jist go through the trees."

We start through the trees with the herd agin. I'm cleanin' the gun and we're on the move. I git the muzzle loader cleaned as best I can and git 'er reloaded and hand it back to Chino. Crash, smash, bang we hear 'em fightin' agin. We're in the middle of 'em agin. We got cows goin' by us. All of a sudden Eight Ball goes by and 'round the tree comes another bull. Chino hauls up and KABOOM shoots a little three-year-old, scrawny, five-by-five, rag-horn bull point blank in the chest. *It's the wrong damn bull.* Little three-year-old bull.

This little bull wheels, spins and charges 'bout thirty yards between me and Chino and piles up. Roberto charges over to the bull and slams him into the ground while this little bull is mortally wounded. Four hundred inches of antler and he grinds that little bull into the dirt. And picks him up. The wounded bull falls off and yells and gits up and tries to run agin. He runs 'bout twenty yards and I'm runnin' through the trees and I'm cleanin' that rifle and I ain't gitin' that rifle clean and that little bull moves out agin. Runs over and falls by a tree. Roberto comes over and hits 'im again. WHAM. And he yells and screams and the lightnin' pops and the thunder crashes and the elk move into the trees.

Roberto slams into that mortally wounded bull, pins 'im down with his horns and shoves 'im up under a tree, picks his hind end up and flips 'im. Now we got eleven hundred pounds o' huge bull elk with four-hundred inches o' horn slammin' into a little bitty, mortally wounded bull that may be two-hundred and sixty inches o' horn and that don't weigh five hundred pounds. That little bull runs over and falls by a tree. He's hurt and he can't get away. And that little, wounded bull struggles to his feet and makes a run for it. He runs 'bout forty yards and falls agin. Roberto comes up and mangles him.

The whole time I'm reloadin' that muzzle loader. I clean that rifle. I git it reloaded YEEE and I burst through the trees and I run up there and stop. Now, addin' insult to injury, I go right by the little bull that's dyin'. He's dyin' and I go right by 'im. No hunter oughta ever walk on by a bull he's jist shot.

Roberto comes 'round the tree looks at me and yells, UUAH. Stands there and jist growls at me, Whrrooww. I stand there lookin' at 'im at fifteen yards with a loaded muzzle-loader in my hands.

I look at 'im and I say, "It's your lucky day." I let 'im walk 'cause I didn't have a tag.

He turns and walks off through the trees. AHHHH. It was one o' the best, one of the toughest hunts I've ever experienced. One o' the greatest flow of more adrenalin than a person is allowed. It was a helluva deal. We harvested the five by five bull. It was a nice bull.

Roberto lived for four more years. A Navajo killed 'im up here. He scored four-hundred fifty-eight inches o' antler and may be the number three bull world record. And I had 'im at fifteen yards broadside and didn't shoot 'im 'cause we'd already killed one. Now a whole lot o' guys would o' shot him and left that little one layin'. Don't think I haven't dreamt 'bout it. Don't think I haven't thought 'bout my decision that day. We should o' killed him. We had 'im. And we didn't. It jist wasn't our day. It jist wasn't our day.

CHAPTER FORTY-TWO
Bare Huntin'

My huntin' partner calls this the time I went bare-huntin' elk. I draw a unit one Arizona archery trophy bull tag. A tag I've always wanted. I've only drawn one in my life. We find this big old bull up there in the trees. He's got 'bout forty cows with 'im. And 'bout five or six, maybe eight satellite bulls runnin' 'round all the time tryin' to steal cows from 'im. So I can't get close to 'im. Every time I start gittin' close a cow finds me or a calf walks up on me. Somethin' goes wrong. So for days I'm tryin' to kill this bull.

One night while we're out in camp, after we were done for the day, my huntin' partner's wife meets us halfway. She brought us a big old pot o' hot, green chili and some beer. I'm kind o' frustrated anyway, so we sit 'round and eat green chili and drink beer 'til way too long in the night. I gotta be up and on the move, on foot, at four a.m. to be in this valley by the time that bull gets there at daylight, 'bout seven. I gotta be movin' at least three hours before daylight to git there. So I jist pull on my camouflage coveralls, 'cause I'm late, a little bit hung over and I'm gittin' outta there.

I hump it up the mountain and I git up there as far as I can git and I git into this valley. It's a deep little rimmed valley. Mountain on one side and meadow on the other. And a real toad come up the valley right as I git there.

Everything's workin' right 'til I gotta git rid o' that green chili. I got a belly full of. I got that big herd comin' right at me and that green chili's leavin' me. And it's leavin' me now! So I climb up next to this rim and the bull's buglin', walkin' above me. I got elk walkin' twenty yards 'bove me. I jerked my coveralls down and git rid o' my bugle, my quiver, all the stuff you gotta carry when you hunt elk. I jerked them coveralls down and I git rid o' that green chili, git cleaned up and the whole time the elk are walkin' by jist 'bove me.

Well, this is where this whole thing gits nasty. I go to pull those coveralls up and when I do that green chili flies agin. I done shit all over the collar o' my coveralls. I got shit up the back o' my neck. All I can smell is shit. I've done ruined everythin' and that bull thunders right 'bove me. Gives a big old bull bugle. Jist can't be fifty yards away. Now I'm in a world o' hurt. So I shuck my boots. I shuck them coveralls. Max, my partner's up on the hill spottin' the herd and stuff wonderin' *where is he? Where the hell is he? He's gotta be right there. Where's he gone?* Now I'm shucked down to my boots and my tan boxers and I grab my bow and my quiver and I busted outta that rim. Left my coverals and everythin' layin' there in a shitty, smelly pile. It's a brisk September morning and I'm skippin' through the dew in the middle o' the elk with nothin' but my boxers on. My partner's a mile away on the rim. He thinks I bust out o' there butt ass naked. He swears to this day I was naked.

There's a satellite bull runs in right as I come up and he peels him a cow off. The herd bull runs over to the other side and they're all kind o' concentratin' on what's goin' on with them and they're not really payin' attention to me. I charge right up there in the middle of 'em and I'm runnin' alongside a satellite bull not twenty yards from me while he's chasin' a cow. The big bull and the rest o' the cows realize they gotta leave; so I'm kinda runnin' right through the middle o' the elk and the big bull eludes my arrow agin. I never fire one on 'im. He keeps outta range. I never git a shot but it was worth a try.

When I git back to my partner, he needs an explanation. So I give him an explanation.

And he said, "Ya know, I guess we're glad you didn't kill 'im or you'd hunted naked the rest o' your life."

So now I take it real easy with the extra-hot, green chili when I gotta leave camp at four a.m.

Chapter Forty-Three
𝑛𝟣𝑇𝑅𝑚

One o' my favorite deals in huntin' was nitrm (nobody in their right mind). I hunt a lot o' country. As you look 'round, you realize nobody in their right mind will git off on foot and go from here to there. So that's what I do. When I figure out that one o' them nitrm's people aren't gonna do that, that's what I do. Those nitrm's have got me in some terrible fixes.

Couple years ago Max and I, we'd come up on Harla Rosa Canyon. It was rainin' hard. We're tryin' to git to our camp and it's a good three miles south o' the canyon. I'd crossed that canyon early in the mornin'. Now it was 'bout seven o'clock at night. Its rainin' hard when we git to the main arroyo. There's water over the top o' the culvert. Water's runnin deep so we pull up there and park. I git out in boot-top water and walk out there 'cross that culvert. Now I'm in knee-deep water.

I walk all the way, 'bout twenty foot, to the other side and say, "Alright, we can make this knee-deep. We can make this."

I walk back the same darn tracks that I took first and git in the truck. "Yeah, we can make it."

We take off in the truck 'cross that culvert. When we cross that culvert, the entire truck just sucks it down. I had walked on a little eddy when it was 'bout two foot wide. If I'd stepped over on this side it was six- to eight-foot deep runnin' sixty miles an hour. Now my partner's had three open-heart surgeries and we're in a world o' hurt. The trucks in the water up to the dash, back end stickin' up in the air and it's stuck in a little eddy.

We climb outta the passenger side door and I git up in the back and git the chains 'n the come-a-longs and we hook it to the culvert. I figure we're gonna lose. This is goin' down stream anytime.

We jack on it and jack on it. Break a couple o' come-a-longs and a handy-man jack. Finally we jist give up and chain it to the culvert. The whole time the water's risin' and it's loud. Them flash floods in arroyos, they're loud. It's rollin' down through there.

I git the brainy idea the camp's jist three mile. And then the Lynch Ranch is only 'nother four mile from there. If I can git to camp, I got a four wheeler there. I can git a truck at the Lynch. So I decide to give it a try. I step out round the front o' the truck and all of a sudden I'm to my armpits. I realize I'm not gonna make it. Then I made a mistake. I turned my body and as I turned my body the water overwhelms ya. When you're sideways ya got a little chance. Turn your back or your front to it, you're done. I tuned my body and as I did I pitched the cell phone and under I went. Down stream I went. High speed.

By then I was downstream fifty yards. Max said he got a little concerned the second time I went under. *I got a little concerned* the second time I went under. I took a deep breath and I let it take me. I thought, *ya know, I better git to shore and I better git there now!* So when I come up the third time I was doin' 'bout sixty miles per hour at least 'bout a hundred yards from the truck. Rollin' in the wake, I come up and charge as hard as I can, give 'bout five big strides toward the shore. When I pull my head up outta that brown, filthy water I see this sorry ass little piece o' sage brush root stickin' outta the bank. I reach up and I grab hold o' that sorry ass piece o' sage brush. It holds. I drag myself on up on that bank.

Nothin's changed. I went for a little swim. It could o' been my last one. But we're still in a world o' hurt. We're on the side of a crick at least twenty miles from the nearest inhabited structure . . . if they're home. I got a sixty-three-year old man with me who's already had at least three heart attacks; it's fadin' to dark and we're in the middle o' nowhere with nothin' but wet clothes and wet boots. I climb a mesa and I git up there and, luckily, that cell phone works. I git a hold o' some Zuni guys that work for me and I give 'em directions. Ed, Edd and Eddy, show up in the middle o' nowheres where we're walkin' down the road in the dark o' the night and they're drunker than hoot owls by the time they git there.

'Nother one o' my philosophies is 'there ain't no such thing as a ugly rescue party.' I don't care what they look like. There ain't no such thing as a ugly rescue party. Ed has the truck, Eddy's supposed to be the brains and Edd's the comedy relief. Well Ed's drivin' and Ed's only got one eye and we got thunderstorms and he ain't got no depth-perception what-so-ever. We're drivin' through flash floods and he can't even see it runnin'. They're all drunker than hell. So we git in with 'em and they give me a ride all the way back. Seventy-five miles of joyous fear.

Chapter Forty-Four
Fame

I been real lucky in my travels in life in that I left here and was able to come back years later and make a livin' where I spent my childhood. Truly blessed. I killed my first deer out here when I was a young boy. To be able to hunt those same ridges is a rarity. I don't think many men get that opportunity.

That opportunity is dwindlin' faster and faster today. It's bein' devastated on several different fronts. Habitat decreases every day for wildlife 'cause people are movin' into country they never used to live in. The anti-fur people. The anti-trap people. They've stopped a whole lot o' predator reduction. Now there's coyotes all the way to New York City. And they never used to be past the Mississippi River. Lion numbers are greater than maybe they've ever been in history.

Outfitters are controllin' big chunks o' land and chargin' big money to hunt big game. It's become a rich man's sport. And we all lose from that. The trophy hunter and the big money guys are quick to bring law suits, are quick to lock gates, quick to deny access. Doesn't have nothin' to do with wildlife. Nothin' to do with conservation. Doesn't have nothin' to do with carryin' on a heritage no matter how many commercials they put on TV. 'Cause these are the same guys that are chargin' nine thousand dollars for an elk hunt. So we all know it's 'bout money. No matter what they say, it's all 'bout them makin' money.

When it comes to a trophy animal, people will cross lines. They'll cross lines of ethics. They'll cross lines of legality. They'll cross lines that the only reason people cross is money. And the record books are full of 'em. Full o' rich men that paid for a record. I have five animals that qualify for the record books. All of 'em have come off public land with general hunting licenses. I've never bothered to enter any of 'em in the record book. It doesn't mean anything to me. What means somethin' to me is the memories o' that hunt and I'll always have those. I don't need my name in 'em.

Had some famous elk hunters from the Rocky Mountain Elk Foundation and stuff come in here and tell me, "We're gonna make you famous."

"I'm already famous."

"No. We're gonna make you *really* famous."

I said, "No, *you* don't git it. I'm already really famous. I can't go in WalMart store anywhere within a hundred miles without someone comin' up and talkin' with me."

"Well, we're gonna put you on TV and stuff."

"Naw. I don't need to be there."

I said, "I've already had my picture in the post office. Where else do ya want it?"

So I never got involved with that. The outfitters, the trophy game hunters in my little niche o' the world, aren't worth the powder to blow 'em to hell. They're a seedy bunch at best and will do whatever it takes to put that money in their wallet. They don't care what it is.

I was raised where, if you killed somethin', you ate it. Up until I killed my first man, I agreed with that.

CHAPTER FORTY-FIVE
Gettin' All Wet

What was that movie? *Crouching Tiger, Hidden Dragon*? Yeah, that was it. The war was over before it ever started. We had a similar war. We call it *The Prayin' Mantis Challenge in the Parkin' Lot*.

Shalako is the Zuni tribe's biggest holiday. It's when their gods come to visit 'em. It's a busy time and people from different tribes, people from all over the world show up to see it. One Shalako weekend, one o' those Saturday nights, a little short guy came in from Hopi. He came in the bar and we had a kind o' loud crowd. We were havin' a good time and he came in askin' directions to Zuni.

Everybody in here was from Zuni and we started teasin' 'im. Well the little guy gits mad and before it's over he's gonna kick everybody's ass in the whole place. He gits into it with a bigger guy named Kary from Zuni. They go out into the parkin' lot all over silliness. I go out there to break it up.

When I git out there I tell Kary: "Knock it off. Go back inside."

All of a sudden this little guy's gonna kick *my* ass. He's standin' in front o' me. I ain't very big myself but this guy can't be four-eleven. He gits down into some sort o' prayin' mantis, Kung Fu karate stance that makes 'im all o' three foot tall.

He's standin' right in front o' me and he goes "AAEEYAH," and gits down into some kind o' comical crouch.

I just reach over, grab him on top o' the head, push 'im down and say, "Don't do that. You'll git hurt. Don't do that."

He got up and ran for his pick-up, got in and left. The poor guy got scared to death. I felt sorry for 'im but I was tryin' to help 'im; but all of a sudden he Kung Fu'd up on me, disappeared, and rode clear outta sight. Prayin' Mantis. Was one o' the funniest things I ever had and we've had a few.

One time I had one little guy come up to the window. By little guys, I mean in height. Zuni and Pueblo Indian men don't have a lot o' height but they have a lot o' girth. He may weight two-ten but he's only five-six.

One day this guy comes up to the window. Little short guy. My drive up window's 'bout four and a half feet off the ground. It's made for a pickup window. Most o' my customers drive pickups and it works out good for me. But this little guy walks up to the window. He's drunker'n hell. He's tryin' to order somethin' to drink.

I tell him, "Nooo. You don't git noth' to drink. You know you're already drunk, Bud."

He starts yellin' at me that I'm racist and stuff and I say, "Nooo, you're jist drunk."

He says, "I'm gonna come inside and kick your ass."

He starts towards the front door and I say, "Wait a minute. Come back here."

He walks back there to the window and looks up at me.

"I'll save you the trouble. I'll save us *both* the trouble. You don't have to walk all the way over there. Let's jist do it right here."

BOOM. I drill 'im as hard as I can. My shoulder's 'bout eight feet off the ground and his head's 'bout five foot. When I drill 'im he just crumbles into a pile right there in front o' the drive-up window.

I saved 'im that long walk. He got up and staggered toward the truck he come out of and off they went.

One night two Zuni guys come in with their girl friends. One of 'em's kind of a racist when he gits drunk. It'd been building' for a while. He's runnin' his mouth. As the evenin' wore on his mouth got 'im in trouble. I finally had 'nough of it and I called 'im on it. I told 'im that was it. I was gonna kick his ass and I went after 'im. I went 'round the bar and as I went 'round the bar, him and his younger, larger brother both jumped up.

I said, "Go on. Git outside. I'm gonna kick both your asses."

So they charge out the door in front o' me. I charge up and I git the door and I jist close and lock that big, heavy, solid wood door.

I come back and sit down between their girl friends 'n ask, "Can't you girls do any better than that? I mean, let's jist think about this."

The two boys are out there yellin' and screamin' insults at me when they realize they're locked out. They're cut off. No more beer, they've done lost their dates, they done lost everything. I sit in here 'n git their girls 'nother beer and left 'em outside. When they was done yellin' I let 'em order what they wanted to go. Then I got the girls what they wanted. We laughed and hee-hawed all the way to the door. I opened up the door and let the girls out and locked it back up. That was the way to handle that.

Had a birthday party in the bar. I had a few friends here, couple o' strangers and 'nother Navajo girl we called Fatal Attraction. Always a little lewd, a little too friendly. Lewd but harmless, or so I thought. We had a birthday party goin' on. Closin' time was comin' up. I was gonna have a little private party after closin' time back in my house. A couple o' my employees were gonna hang back. Fatal Attraction invited herself. Decided she was gonna stay. So I went 'round the bar and sat between her and her girl friend.

I sat down and told 'em, "You girls gotta go, you know. It's closin' time."

"No, I'm gonna stay."

"No, you gotta go."

She got up behind me and went towards the door. I jist looked back at the TV. I thought she was leavin'. I was sittin' there with a drink in one hand and a cigarette in the other and all of a sudden my whole body jolted. I'm sittin' here on a stool facin' the bar and she gits up and goes behind me to leave and gits back there and, BOOM, plants a haymaker right below my ear. Right in the bottom o' the jawbone. Puffs it all up. 'Bout three weeks o' ringin' in that ear. If a man would o' hit me like that it would o' knocked me out cold. She gave me her best shot and it was a helluva shot. I'll give the girl credit for it.

I was stunned. Cigarette went rollin' across the bar, my drink tipped over, knocked my hat off. It was a three or four second delay 'til the lights came back on. I looked and figured *what's my cigarette rollin' across the bar for? Wait'll I git my drink off my hat.* OK I picked my hat up, picked my cigarette up looked up and then I thought, *that bitch hit me and she hit me hard.*

I realized when she'd gone behind me she planted her feet and threw a big right hook that hit me under the bottom of the ear and *rang my bell.*

I got up and I said, "Bitch, you hit me. What fuckin' boardin' school'd you learn that in?" I was a little ticked off.

About that time, my barmaid Carrie, she comes outta the back room like a locomotive. She is smokin' outta there. She has got her right arm cocked and she is comin' full speed.

Now this girl's kind o' political. So I git in between and I say, "No, no, Carrie. Let her go."

'Nother girl we call Scrapper comes outta the back room; gits to the doorway before the Navajo girl who's backin' away from me, retreatin' from my advance. Scrapper got to the door first.

She said, "You hit Gary. I'm gonna kick your ass."

Scrapper was gonna clean her up so I gotta reach 'round the Navajo girl to get Scrapper outta the doorway so I can git her out the door. When I reach 'round to remove Scrapper POW that bitch nails me agin. Hits me right in the nose and I'm tryin' to save her life.

I said, "Do you think that hurt? I got a seven-year-old hits harder than that," which was all a bluff 'cause it hurt like hell. I had blood runnin' outta my nose. I'd been nailed twice by a girl who knew how to fight.

I step back in the door and say, "That's it girls. Kick her ass," on account o' she hit me in the nose right in the door.

One time I had to throw a girl named Rose out. Rose was a problem child. She was in the back room raisin' hell and the girl wouldn't leave. Every time I git near, she's kickin' and punchin' on me. So finally she sits down in the middle o' the floor back there and just kicks at anything that goes by. She's spinnin' 'round and kickin' on the floor back there and I'm mad. I've taken several hits from this girl. Finally I jist pick her up in a cradle with her feet stickin' out and I carry her out the door.

When I git out the door I'm mad and I'm lookin' for some place to set the girl down. There's a big old mud puddle out there and I walk out there in the middle o' that parkin' lot and I jist drop her right in the middle o' that mud puddle. WHAP and I step back.

A woman jumps out of a car and says, "Don't you hit that woman."

"Hit her? Hell, I'm tryin to turn her loose."

One time I had a guy take a swing at me out in the parkin' lot and I'm mad. I'm already mad anyway. I got horse shit goin' on. Pushin' and shovin' and drunks in the doorway and I'm mad. I go out there and a guy goes down. He's layin' out there and they're tellin' me he's got a ride in a white pickup. I pick im up and I heave 'im up over my shoulder.

I'm carryin' 'im to the back o' the pickup truck and his feet are stickin' out and I'm lookin' and all of a sudden I see water runnin' out o' his pant legs. Only it ain't water he's peein' out o' the ends o' his pants. I got 'im on my shoulder and I'm carryin' 'im and all of a sudden BOOM, I launched 'im like any male cheerleader would be proud of and I pitched that body all the way to the back o' the dam truck.

I say, "Bud, I'm tryin' to help you out and you're pissin' on me."

Chapter Forty-Six

Nearly Missin'

My first muzzle-loader antelope hunt I had thirteen or fourteen antelope bonus points. That means I haven't drawn an antelope tag in thirteen or fourteen years. They're hard to draw here at home in northern Arizona.

So finally I drew a muzzle loader antelope tag. Down by the power plant, eighteen miles south o' the bar there's a big buck. He's runnin' with 'bout a dozen does. I watch 'im all summer. I know other guys are seein' 'im, too, but I don't realize at the time how many hunters there are 'round the power plant. It's a big thing in this country and I don't realize they're all watchin' 'im too. Openin' mornin' I pull in there. I git at the gate 'n there's a truck in there goin' in jist in front o' me.

I'd seen this antelope and his herd the night before. They were in the flat 'bout a mile from the road, between me and the railroad track. So I jist pull the truck off by the gate and I grab my muzzle-loader and jump up into some real rough little clay banks. I run down there and drop down into the bottom of an arroyo and go down that arroyo in the dark o' the night. I jist git to that arroyo and I hear chik-boom. A muzzle-loader goes off. It's still in the dark. It ain't light enough to shoot yet and I hear this muzzle loader go off and I thought *damn they poached that sucker right in front o' me. They poached that sucker.*

I jist keep on boogyin' down that arroyo. I git down there a ways and all of a sudden I look up and there's this doe goin' by me. Goin' right by me and it starts gittin' daylight. I look up and that buck's followin' her. The day before the hunt he'd got in a fight with another buck and broke his tips off. That cost him some in the record book but he was still a helluva buck. I still wanted 'im so I pulled up, jist at daylight, and he walks by. He's just walkin' with his head down followin' that doe. Doesn't even see me. I pull that muzzle loader up and kelliick. Durin' my hustle down the arroyo the percussion cap on my muzzle-loader had wiggled loose so when I dropped the hammer on it, it smashed sideways on the nipple and never fired. And they went on by.

I drop back down in the bottom o' that arroyo and I boogy and I boogy and I boogy and git down in there to where that arroyo was only 'bout three feet deep. Now I'm in the sage brush and I come out o' that arroyo right in the middle o' that herd, so I lay there. Jist lay there on the ground. I got three does watchin' me. They're standin' there lookin' at me and they're not fifteen yards away. And I keep waitin', keep waitin', keep waitin'. Finally them does give up on me. They moved and start grazin'. I raised up outta that sage brush and there he is, standin' with thirteen does. He's 'bout sixty yards away.

I touch one off and bounce it right off the top o' his shoulders and the race is on. Whole herd takes off full speed. By now I'm clear out in the flat. I take off up to the ridges and I go down to the ridges. Those antelope make a big circle out through there. I git up to a point where I think I can ambush 'em. I come down on that point and they come out but they come out 'bout two hundred yards out there so I wait.

There's an arroyo they gotta cross and as they cross it that antelope comes up that arroyo. He's almost perpendicular and way out there. I got no range finder in those days so I touch one off. tawhoomph KAWACK.

I begin one o' the ugliest kills I've ever had in my life. I take his right hind leg off just at the knee. Off they go agin out through the flat. I pick up my loader. Now when I left the truck I loaded that muzzle loader and I had three speed loaders with me. That's all I had for ammo and that was my second round. Now I got an antelope with one hind leg blown off at the knee and a big gash through the top o' his shoulders.

I take out 'cross the flat with 'im and I stay in that arroyo, git down there a ways, and he's slowin' down. He's hurt but a hurt antelope can still do thirty-miles-an-hour. I ease up through the sage brush. When I raise up to shoot he bolts. He's goin' away from me and I need to git more lead in him. I touch one off and KAWHACK I take his other hind leg off. Now this is torturin' him and torturin' me. I take off agin. He's goin' as hard as he can. He's runnin' on his hams. He still can out run my ass. He's runnin' on his hind knees and he's boogyin. So I git reloaded and I git up as close as I can to 'im and he's runnin' 'bout a hundred yards away and KAPOW, I fire my last round. And I hear 'im thoomp.

But he takes off and he charges up over this little hill leavin' me standin' here. OK so I'll catch my breath here. He's gotta go down. I've just gotta give 'im time now. I'm gonna have to go back to the truck and I've gone five miles, six miles maybe now in a short period o' time. We've covered some distance out on the flat and I can taste blood. I ain't in near good 'nough shape for that run.

I'm standin' there re-groupin' and I hear kaacheeTHOOM. I hear this muzzle-loader go off and I charge up that hill. I look and there's a guy walkin' down through the trees. I see my antelope strugglin' down the draw. He's still movin' on his hams. I bust and run as hard as I can and I tackle that antelope. KABLAM, I body slam that antelope hold him down good cuttin' his throat.

Two guys walk up. I said, "This is my antelope."

They say, "We know. Been watchin' you for five miles. We're jist tryin' to help you out." one says, "You're Witch Well aren't cha?"

"Yeah, I guess I am."

"Well come on. We gotta go find 'nother antelope" and off they went.

This was a muzzle-loader trophy book antelope and they were kind o' mad at me. I was mad at me, too, but what I found out later was there was a guy on every one o' them ridge points. There were at least five guys out there tryin' to git to that antelope when I raise up in the middle of them and shot 'im.

CHAPTER FORTY-SEVEN
Thieves

Earl Keyes was full o' stories. Earl claimed he was in almost two hundred movies as an extra. Claimed he was close friends with Errol Flynn, or one of 'em. And he was close friends with Bruce Wayne who played Batman. This guy was the actor's buddy. Claimed one o' the dogs he had out on his forty had belonged to Wayne. What was that guy's real name? I don't remember if that was his character's name or his real one.

One time while Earl was here, I had a Zuni guy come in with an old pot he wanted to sell me. It was an old piece o' pottery and I bought it off the guy. He don't know nothin'. Gave them twenty bucks.

Earl realizes I might buy some o' that old stuff. The next day he comes in with a pipe. A rock pipe he said he'd dug up on his property. The pipe was in the shape of a frog. A fetish type pipe. I liked the pipe and I picked it up and smelled it. It was cherry blend.

Now if a guy don't know what he's doin' you can buy them matatas and bowls and artifacts in Mexico all day long for five bucks. They'll make you whatever you want right out back there while you wait. And that's what he'd brought me in. He'd brought me in one o' them Mexican pipes that he was tryin' to pass off as an antique, as an artifact'. I asked him if he had any more o' that cherry blend 'cause that's all that pipe was worth, to smoke out of.

He always had an angle. Always had an angle. He had Elvis' plates or somethin'. He had a couple gold plates. Solid gold 'cordin' ta him. I looked at 'em a couple o' times and they weren't gold. They were cloisonne. He thought they were a bunch o' money. He was always tryin' to sell somthin' for his drink. And you never knew where he picked it up.

Chapter Forty-Eight
Leave The Dead Lay

Witch Well is surrounded by artifacts. This country we live in, the high plateau, the high desert has been inhabited for thousands o' years. They kind o' look at these artifacts as whether they're Folsom, Anasizi, or Zuni.

When I was younger we found a ruin. Some of us Cub Scouts found a ruin. At first it fascinated me. Then I forgot all 'bout it. When I moved back down here it was big business. People were diggin' pots everywhere. Since then the laws have changed to tighten a lot o' that up; but when I came back here it was big business. People were gittin' shot over it.

They dug up some kivas down here. Three or four o' them forty acre maggots. Ray Scott, Bob Dodge, couple others. One of 'em was a Vaughn or somethin'. Anyway four of 'em dug them things up and they dug up some Pueblo fetish gods 'n Zuni gods. One of 'em run off and sold 'em in New York. There were seven o' them little dolls. Little rock fetish dolls. It took the Zunis a long time to get 'em back but they did finally git 'em back.

As far as grave diggers, I figured they got what was comin' to 'em. 'Cause within four years they were all of 'em dead. All of 'em. Outta them four guys I think they were all dead in four years. They had gun fights over them damn things, over who got the money and who didn't git the money.

It's always kind o' dicy comin' up on these pot diggers. My wife and I tracked some of 'em into New Mexico onto my neighbor's ranch. We come up on a mesa. Once I got to where they were I knew what they were doin'. I knew they were headed to some ruins. We pulled up there and my wife stayed in the truck.

I got out and yelled "Hello the truck."

A guy come up over the rim and he was sixty years old and had a thirty year old boy with 'im. The thirty year old boy was carryin' a big old Dan Wesson 44 pistol from what I could guess from lookin' at it.

I ask 'em, "What the hell you boys doin' in here?"

"Oh, we're scoutin' for deer."

I said, "That's damn funny 'cause lottery results hasn't even been announced yet. You're scoutin' for deer in this unit and we don't know who's got a tag and who doesn't?"

"Well, uh," the young one, he moves his hand toward the butt of that pistol, says, "Uh, what're you gonna do 'bout it? Ain't none o' your business."

I tell him, "You guys are diggin' pots. You git your asses outta here. NOW."

He puts his hand on his pistol. "What're you gonna do 'bout it?"

I said, "I'm gonna run your dam asses outta here, like I said. Now git in your dam truck and git the hell outta here."

I could tell he wanted to raise that pistol up. I could tell it was gittin' dicy.

Just then that sweet little wife o' mine steps outta the truck with an m-16, jacks one in it and says, "You *will* do what he says and you will *do it now!*"

By god there's sound advice in not arguin' with a woman with an assault rifle in her hands. They did 'xactly what she said. Her timin' could not be better. 'Cause this boy is 'bout to show the ugly side o' life. He was 'bout to show that I could not run 'im off. I had measured the distance between him and I and calculated whether I could take 'im down before he could hit me with that thing but she solved that problem.

You never know with these forty acre maggots. I caught some on the south end o' my ranch. I didn't exactly catch 'em but I found their camp. They had a lean-to with a smudge pot out there. Had a white camper door on the lean-to.

When I found the camp, I got a black magic marker from my truck and I wrote on that camper door: *No grave diggin'. Violators will be shot. Survivors will be fed to my dog.*

I left that sign for 'em. And I came back and called a deputy sheriff to report them.

Chapter Forty-Nine

Native Names

Hirin' and firin' Bartenders and Barmaids is the worst part o' this whole job. I've had some good ones. I had a Kentucky trapper named Tim stayed with me several years and we remain friends to this day. He settled in this country after he'd left me. He's a good man and stayed a long time. I had an old girl from Rock Ridge named Elaine Jackson, A sweetheart. Everybody's friend. Absolutely color blind. Did all she could for people. Remembered everybody's name. That's quite a trick. I've known a couple of 'em. I had one named Dixie. Lesbian girl lived with me. 'Nother sweetheart. Good women, her 'n her partner, Sue.

I had an old girl come outta Phoenix named Johnnie, stayed 4 years and she was good help. But there've been times I've gone through thirteen in a year. There've been several who didn't make it a day.

While back I've got a job application out. I was takin' job applications and here's what I got to choose from. My huntin' partner for one thing. He asked me to hire his daughter-in-law. She's on parole. Got five years o' community service facin' her. Husband in prison. She's known 'bout the job for a week. Has talked to me on the phone three times but I've told 'er she has to come out here for an interview and show me she wants the job. She's gotta come out here and so far she's known 'bout it five days and I still haven't seen 'er. She's not high on my list.

Recently my first applicant was a twenty-seven-years old, plump Zuni girl. Party girl. P-aaa-r-teee girl. Her last job was five years ago as a nurses' aid. Never run a cash register before. Never worked behind a counter.

Barb, I let go 'cause she's light fingered. She wants her job back. Well I can't afford her. A guy named Harvey, a Navajo guy. Lives up here in the New Lands. He's twenty one years old. He's a regular. Runs with a rough crowd. Way too young and inexperienced ta start with.

And we got a new forty-acre maggot. Bought the trailer park down the road. The RV park. Him and his partner live down there. Has experience as a bartender and he lists that he worked for a bar for two years and the reason for leavin' is that the bar closed down. I never liked the guy. He knows it. He commented that I didn't like 'im and I told 'im he was perceptive.

Ok and, uh, Carrie, my number-one barmaid's girlfriend. This is not gonna work. This'n workin' days, the other'n workin' nights. She's one o' the Zuni Ola Maidens. She's gone 'round the world dancin' from time to time on tour. Jist got back from Mongolia. So I'm not hirin' one that's gonna be gone a month from now.

'Nother applicant, ex-con, Navajo, lives up in the New Lands. Drinks eight or nine forties a day. Makes three trips a day to git two or three forties o' Malt Liquor. Not an option. Would not mix well with others.

The only other one I got is Teri, and that's prob'ly what I'm hirin'. Worked for me one day one time before. She has come out twice since the job came open so she's tryin' for the job. She's a party girl. Some o' the girls that work 'round here and Teri don't necessarily git 'long too well. Teri's prob'ly got a drug problem.

So out o' my applications I've got; I got two party girls, one of 'em with no experience whatsoever, one of 'em maybe tryin' to straighten up. I got one on parole and one just outta prison, the one on parole doin' five years o' public service. I got a nine-forties-o-malt-liquor-a-day customer, ya know? I got a twenty-one-year-old gang banger with no experience... wannabe gang banger. I got a California forty-acre maggot that I neither trust nor like. I got a ex-employee I fired for bein' a thief and wants her job back That's not gonna happen.

So jist what am I supposed to hire from? Employees have always been a battle. Always been a battle. Some of 'em'll really hurtcha. This job runnin' a bar in the middle o' the Arizona high desert plateau thirty miles from the nearest town isn't all glamour.

Out here when they become an employee you share bathrooms. You share meals. You share your lives to some extent. It's workin' in tight quarters. If you work here for me you're part o' the family. If I can't trust ya, you don't work here long

I set traps. I'm the trapinest son-of-a-gun that ever walked. When I distrust someone I set traps. My employees know it. I set all kinds o' traps. I count certain things from day to day. I walk in and read the tape in front of 'em. When I have one I distrust I ketch 'em every time. Even though they know I set traps, they can't resist. I count bottles. I move things 'round. I tear little slips o' paper and hide 'em in corners to see if they're moved or not. I do all kinds o' little things. Prob'ly twisted o' me to do that but it's the only way I can ketch 'em. I'm not gonna sit here for hours nor am I gonna pay for expensive equipment to view 'em. That's a little beyond your rights o' privacy. I have cameras in here. Oh yeah, there's cameras in here. There's been a camera in here for years . . . there's cameras in here and outside and I have monitors. I leave 'em on, on the outside cameras. But when I've got the girls workin', I don't sit and watch the girls. I don't sit and watch the employees, male or female.

Over the last few years, Carrie, (my current and favorite bar maid) and I took to giving the other bar maids Super Secret Indian Names. For instance:

My best one: Smiles With Teeth
Girl of conviction: Kachina Hair Woman
An ex-stripper: Dazed Beaver,
A gorgeous Zuni: Dazed Beaver Two,
A hippy: Keeps Tipi Down Wind,
A naive one: Head Whistles With Wind
A freckled bartender: Speckled Bellied Squaw Hopper
A big girl: Two Seasons Woman, warmth in winter, shade in summer.
They call me: Chief Speaks From Behind

Chapter Fifty
Justice Self Served

Well, back in '99 I bought a Ford truck: green, one-ton, power-stroke, 4-wheel-drive. Nice truck. I took it up to Gallup one day to git a bed liner and headin' rack. Go down to Gallup Weldin' and its kind o' rainin' and drizzlin' that day. I noticed a little Ford Bronco for sale over on the street so I left my truck there at Gallup Weldin' and walked over and got the phone number off that little Ford Bronco. Thought it'd be another give-a-way ride for my next promotion at the bar. I go over there to Allsup's to call on the north side o' Gallup and I try to make a couple phone calls, can't get either guy. So I'm leanin' there 'gainst the buildin'

I never dress up for Gallup. Well I never dress up period, but I never dress up for Gallup. So I'm leanin' over there on Allsup's with my variety coat on and my holey blue jeans and the winos start surroundin' me and they start tellin' me the best shelters.

"Hey Bud, you just hang with us, ya know. Don't go over near them nuns, they're mean. There's the third street shelter. We'll go over there and have lunch. They got good food, ya know."

One of 'em looks at me and says: "Hey, want to go together on a 40 o' malt liquor?"

I looked at 'im and said, "Well, how much you got?"

He says, "I got a dollar fifty."

I said, "Well I don't think I have enough to cover the rest. We can't prob'ly go together on a 40."

Here I am leanin' 'gainst this buildin' surrounded by the homeless and I don't dare reach for a cigarette. I don't dare to reach for change to make 'nother phone call or anything. They figure they got jist 'nother homeless guy. I'm leanin' up here and I prob'ly got three grand in my pocket 'cause I was gittin' work done on the truck and everything else and they're all gonna take me to a shelter for lunch. And I could stay with 'em. They'd take me through the night and I could stay with 'em and they'd show me the best shelters to stay in at night. They were gonna take care o' my sorry homeless ass from leanin' up 'gainst the buildin' in the rain.

Gallup, New Mexico. Drunk City USA. If ya can't find it on the New Mexico map, you jist lift up the tail and it's right underneath. I tell you, that's where you'll find Gallup, New, Mexico.

My hired hand, Tim, and I used to go up there to git supplies. So we go to Gallup Lumber and we git all loaded up, lumber, plywood and everything and we go over to the mall. Tim needed a pair o' boots. He wants to go to K-mart. We pull up there. We git outta the truck. When we git outta the truck I see a Navajo sittin' 'cross starin' at me so I give this guy my number two dirty look and I walk on in with Tim.

'Bout the time I git to the door at K-mart, I tell Tim, "You go on and look for your boots, I'm goin' back to the truck."

By the time I git back to the truck they're unloadin' that shit off my truck. Them two Navajo boys are unloadin' my friggin' truck as fast as they can into their truck in the parkin' lot at the mall. Tim comes runnin out, he's changed his mind. 'Bout the time he got to the boots he realized what was goin' on. So we git in my truck and we chase these guys and they go over to the old Walmart.

They're goin' 'round and 'round in the parkin' lot and we're goin' 'round and 'round tryin' to catch 'em. Finally they line out and they git over there by Napa and I run 'em off the road and I run 'em up on the bank at Napa. They git out and they start makin' a run for it.

I hold 'em there and I tell Tim: "You go call the law."

The law shows up and in the meantime we're unloadin' all my lumber and everything back into my truck.

The cop says, "Well, this is a citizen's arrest. We didn't catch 'em, you got everything loaded back in your truck so if you want these guys arrested you're gonna have to come down and file a complaint and that'll be twenty dollars and then we'll have to keep your stuff until trial."

I said, "You mean I gotta go pay to have this son-of-a-bitch arrested for stealin' all this shit out o' my truck and he's gonna go back to Lucachuki or wherever the hell he's from? He ain't never gonna show up and you're gonna keep my shit?

"Well, yeah. This's a citizen's arrest."

I said, "Alright. Let me think 'bout it a minute."

The guy's leanin' 'gainst his truck. 'Gainst the back o' his truck. So I walk back up there and I lean next to him.

I said, "You know, you're the sorriest mother fucker I've ever seen. You're lucky I don't kick the fuckin' shit outta you 'cause that's gonna be the only justice done here today."

I look back, and the cop, he's standin' there writin' down license numbers and he's not lookin' at anything.

I said, "Aw, the hell with it."

BOOOOOOM. I nailed him right in the eye socket with my elbow jist as hard as I could. KAWACK Down he went.

I looked at my hired hand and I said, "That's alright, Tim, git in the truck we're leavin'." Tim, he's lookin' at me. We git in the truck ya know and we start drivin' away and the cop looks at us and waves. I look back at the other man and here's this guy layin' in the ditch He's gittin' up and he's pointin' at me and I'm goin' on down the street. We drive off and that cop's jist shakin' his head and that was the only justice could be done that day. But justice was served. 'Bout two months later. I walked in Walmart and here's this same guy at customer service center.

I walk right up to 'im and I say "Hey everybody, see this guy right here? He's a thief. If you got anything in your truck you better go out and check it right now. Take a good look at 'im.

I want security. You got cameras? This is a thief."

I yelled, "Anybody know that son-of-a-bitch?" and he ran out the door o' Walmart.

Ya know, I've never been very eloquent. I'm in Phoenix. Pull up at a gas station, Circle K. Here comes a homeless guy up to me. He's got a turquoise ring he'll trade for a drink. Like, duh. Like I don't see any turquoise up here.

So he comes up "Hey buddy, ya wanna buy this ring?"
I looked at him and I said "Git a job."
He says, "Who the fuck's gonna hire me? Jist look at me. Ain't nobody gonna hire me. I can't git a job here. Just look at ya."
I looked at 'im and he was right. Wasn't anybody gonna hire his ass. He didn't have chance one o' gitten a job.
He says, "What kind o' job am I gonna do? Turnin' burgers 3.50 an hour? Man, hell, I can't live on that. All that'll do is let me starve a little slower."
I never did buy that ring but that homeless s.o.b. embarrassed the hell outta me. He jist told me, *look at me. Ain't anybody gonna give me a job.* He was right. There wasn't any arguin' with him.

A few years back we had a mule deer run over down here by the S curve not far from the bar. Nice buck, but a car'd hit him. He wasn't tore up real bad. Some Zuni guys wanted him. The law says you have to have a transport permit from the highway patrol before you can take a road kill. So I call the Highway patrol and then we wait and we wait. 'Bout an hour'd gone by and they ain't never showed up.

Finally the highway patrol shows up and there's me and 'bout seven Indian boys standin' 'round this mule deer killed here. He looks at us like he's George Armstrong Custer. He jist drives on by. He don't wanna stop 'cause it's all red skin standin' there ya know. So he jist drives on by. Don't give us a permit. Don't stop or nothin'. So I think *I gotta git the guts outta this thing.* I pull out my little pocket knife and I open it up. I go to rippin' this deer.

One o' them Zuni guys says, "Zing, that knife's sharp."
I hold up the knife and say, "Let this be a lesson to ya. A Navajo, he can't stab ya, he done pawned his knife. A Mexican, he'll stab ya with a dull knife. He's *always* fuckin with it so it's dull. A Zuni, he's got a sharp knife but it's layin' on a work bench next to that Kachina he ain't finished in three weeks. Now a redneck, he's good to have 'round cause he's got a sharp knife."

Chapter Fifty-One
Pretty is Painful

Of all my employees, the good lookin' ones have been as much trouble as they've been worth. Your average old girl jist tryin' to make a livin' and stuff, they do better. Them super models, them good lookin' ones, they're more trouble than they're worth.

I've never had one last more'n 'bout six months. Oh sure, they bring the dogs 'round but then the dogs gotta pee on everything. That's just the way life is. Good lookin' women tend to think they're better than the rest of us. Life has been easier for 'em. They've been forgiven. The rest of us, our mistakes aren't forgiven but for some reason good-lookin' women don't have to pay for their mistakes.

I had an ex-stripper from California livin' out here in the trees. When I hired her I didn't figure it'd last very long and it didn't. But I had her workin' here for a while 'cause my number one barmaid wound up in jail agin. They'd let me bail her out twice but the third time they kept her. Wouldn't let me bail her out the third time. So I hired this stripper and she was a *stripper*. She'd git up on this counter top and bend over and dust bottles that were on the top shelf. Bent over with her g-strings showin' in front o' the whole crowd.

She'd point her ass and shake her titties every chance she got. Business picked up a little. But she would serve a guy as long as he was tippin' her. She would serve him till he fell off the stool. She got two or three o' my regular customers nailed for DWI within' two months. Many times I warned her 'bout it in the six months she worked for me. I had to fight four or five different times.

One time five Navajos pulled up and I was in back.

She comes back and says, "Gary, I got some problem children."

So I come out and there's three guys in the back room.

I say, "What's up?"

She says, "Well, two of 'em were too drunk to serve so I sent two out and I served these others but these others are trouble."

I said, "What the hell did you serve any of 'em for? They all came together. Two of 'em were too drunk. Jist send 'em all off."

I walked back there and I said, "Hi."

I looked at 'em and they were trouble. That's all there was to that. So I came back and I sat down in my usual chair and talked to some regulars.

One of 'em come up front and ordered three shots o' Jack Daniels.

I walked up to 'em and said, "No, guys, you've had too much. Finish up what beers you got 'n take on off. You prob'ly had too much."

I came back and sat down and 'bout that time one of 'em came in from the outside, one o' them that she'd said was too drunk to serve. He came in and walked to the back room.

The one that had jist ordered the shots, he yells at me, "Hey you fuckin' cocksucker give me four shots o' Jack right now!"

I got up and went towards him and I said, "What did you say to me?"

He said, "I said, hey, you fuckin' cocksucker . . .," and I hit him.

I went over the top o' the bar and nailed him with a hard right in the teeth. He went all the way back to the pool table.

I slid down off the top o' the bar, landed on my feet and said. "You guys git the hell outta here or I'm gonna fuck you up."

One of 'em threw a pool cue at me and I moved and the cue come sailin' by.

I said, "That's it. I'm gonna gitcha."

I came to git my can o' bear stop and another one threw a cue just as I came a runnin'. I caught it, got my bear stop and came 'round the bar.

"I'm gonna mess you up."

As I went 'round, they all ran outside. I git out there and the tough one charged. So I maced 'im. Maced 'em all.

Chapter Fifty-Two
We're All Family

Carries's as good a bar maid as I've ever had. Great sense o' humor tries to do the right thing. Makes good decisions most o' the time behind the bar, in the bar. There's a lot o' Carrie. Carrie's a healthy girl and she's not ashamed of it. She enjoys it. She has fun with it. One day her girl friend said they should exercise. Get in shape.

Carrie said, "I'm already in shape. Round is a shape."

She ain't 'fraid to git out and scuffle with 'em and I chew her out for it. It's not her place but she's been out there a time or two and that's jist Carrie. Jovial, lovin', wonderful Carrie. She has a sense o' humor that doesn't quit She'll drive over mine any day. Sometimes she takes it too far. Does not quit. But I think her humor lightens jist 'bout everybody she meets.

I still remember that little eight-year-old girl peakin' 'round the corner at me when I see Carrie. Carrie's grandfather worked for my father and then leased the bar and stayed here for 'bout fifteen years. Name was Wendell and he had far more interestin' stories to tell than I ever did. But Wendell was a good man. The whole time he leased the bar from my father he was never a day late or a dollar short. That says a lot 'bout a man.

He was a legend when I came here, but now we're a whole different generation. Now the kids that were twenty-one years old when I got here are forty-one years old. It's a whole different world. The stories of Wendell we don't hear anymore like we used to hear.

One o' Wendell's best stories was one time the AIM (American Indian Movement) boys came up. Ervin Wasita, Ernie Mackle and Wendell were here. They were sons-in-law o' Wendell. Two station wagon loads of 'em pulled up. They were gonna git old Wendell 'cause he was a white man sellin' liquor to the Indians.

I don't know what all, whatever happened but Ernie come up over the roof with a M-16 and Ervin come up out by the pump house with another M-16 and Wendell come outta the drive up window with a couple big hand guns. They all let loose. Well they shot 'em a station wagon to the ground. Wendell and the boys did, and the rest o' them AIM boys all jumped in the other one and headed down the road in a limpin' car.

Our local Baptist Minister had heard all the shootin'. In them days he wasn't all that far outta the navy. He come chargin' up here, gun in hand, to see what the war was all 'bout. Them guys had left in such a hurry that there was a box of ammo and two pistols still layin' in the parkin' lot that they had dropped. They'd been tryin' to reload but they were way over-gunned.

That was the end o' the big AIM uprisin' at Witch Well. Those AIM guys came through here in the early seventies 'n stirred some people up and some of it was right and some of it was wrong. That was jist the sign o' the times.

Wendell was not beyond pullin' out a gun and pullin' the trigger indoors. Now I've done it and I don't recommend it. Well, that was how Wendell solved a problem if things got wild and wooly. Wendell jist pulled out a gun and punched another hole in the roof. That was Wendell's style. It worked for him. As for me and indoor firearms, I disagree with, but that's the way Wendell handled things.

Carrie is third generation at Witch Well. She's as much a part o' this place now as anybody could be. Her grandmother worked here. Her mother and father worked here. Now Carrie works here.

When she first came back from California I found out she was workin' up at the video store at the mall or somethin' so I went over to Zuni and offered her a job. She'll be five years here now. We haven't been without our trials and tribulations. Like I said I've bailed her out twice and the third time they wouldn't let me.

I hadn't seen her for a long time while she was in jail and I found out that she was gittin' to do work release at the reservation trash transfer station. 'Bout that time I had a new win-me ride, a little Chevy S10 pickup for next year's bar promotion. I went to the transfer station to see Carrie while she was in jail. I hadn't seen her in a couple months so there she was at the transfer station when I pulled up. And she didn't recognize this little truck. Wondered who that was. I pulled up there and got out and she saw it was me and old Carrie rumbles down the hill to me and her tears began to flow and we gave each other big hugs. Tears start to flow outta my eyes, too.

I pushed her back in that orange jump suit at the dump and I said. "I'm not crying 'cause I'm sentimental. My eyes are waterin' cause o' the smell o' that jump suit"

Then I waited for her to come back to work. Well she did her time in jail 'n then let me know she was out agin.

I still had the stripper workin' for me but I wasn't happy with things. That stripper was a pain in the ass. A good lookin' pain. Helluva body but, in my opinion, had that California mentality that you wait on a customer and you'll never see him again. Out here, we're small town. You gotta take care of 'em. You gotta keep 'em alive. You gotta help 'em out. You want that guy back. You got a limited pool. This ain't California. You can't piss a guy off 'n never see him again and not hurt your wallet. So you gotta explain what happens sometimes to some people. That's why you can't be wishy washy.

I've told people. "Hey this may be a mistake but I'm gonna do it anyway. It's what I've decided to do."

And that's jist the way you gotta approach things. Carrie loves me dearly and I love her. She would lay down her life for me. I would never put her in that situation. But that's what I mean 'bout when you work here, you work here a while, we become family.

Now that has been betrayed. I had a guy that worked here a long time and then he started takin' advantage. He started treatin' this place like it was his, not mine. He's tradin' pussy for beer and runnin' an illegal pawn operation. I talked to 'im two or three times and I was gittin' tired of it and he was livin' here. He was livin' high on the hog. Moved his whole family in at one point and things started comin' up missin'. He was burnin' me bad when I finally got rid o' him. Sometimes you let people into your heart and they take advantage so you try to guard that as much as you can.

Chapter Fifty-Three
Don't Eat the Mint

When I first got here and started fixin' up the place I built a couple bathrooms. I had the men's outside and the women's inside 'cause in them days we had big crowds. Sometimes there'd be a hundred and fifty people here, and jist three or four of us workin' here, mainly girls. It'd be real busy so I had the men's outside and the women's inside. I finally had to lock that outside bathroom up 'cause in three years I replaced seven toilets in that bathroom. They would break that son-of-a-gun up every chance they got.

Old Bee, one of our regular customers, was a real party girl. One day she was sittin' there at the end o' the bar tryin' to git some guy to buy her a beer. Two Navajos walked in. Navajo cowboys. They were in an ornery mood. Old Bee was flirtin' with 'em tryin' to git 'em to buy her a beer.

One of 'em, just outta plumb orneryness, says, "I buy you a beer, you suck my dick."

Well Debbie overheard him say that. And pretty soon, him and Bee, they go outside to the bathroom out there. Go outside anyway. I don't actually know where they went. Then 'bout five minutes later, they come walkin' back in. Bee's rubbin' her mouth when she comes walkin' back in.

They walk up and he says, "Give her a beer."

Debbie says, "Git your sorry asses outta my bar." She run all three of 'em out. Made her so damn mad.

One time I go outside and I'm pickin' up trash and I'm up on the the hill. I'm pickin' up bottles and stuff that they threw 'round. As I come back down the hill I see Debbie and Russ and a couple other guys all standin' around lookin' at the men's bathroom door.

I said, "What's goin' on?"

They said, "You're in the bathroom."

I said, "I am? What am I doin' in the bathroom?"

"Well you're in the bathroom with Bee. They came in and told us you gave her two hundred dollars for sex in the bathroom."

We stood there and watched. Pretty soon the bathroom door opens and she come outta there with a Navajo cowboy. So I guess that gives me 'nother of my lifes' theories. All us cowboys look alike.

I had to inform 'em if I was ever gonna pay for sex for two-hundred dollars I wanted it at the top o' the MGM Grand. I want it for the whole evenin'. I wanna take my time with some bubble bath. It ain't gonna be a couple o' minutes in the john at Witch Well.

I built the dam urinal out of a piece of 'luminum duct work that I sealed up with rubber plastic fiber roof cement. It was as rank as any john around. To clean it out I'd open it up and throw a two gallon bucket o' hot bleach water in it. Then I'd stand back with a hose and clean it out.

One time I went in that bathroom and I closed the door so I could sweep behind the door and there was six-hundred and eleven dollars. In *cash*, layin' behind the door. Evidently a guy had dropped it outta his pocket when he went in. Then when he left, the money slid behind the door. They'd left the door open. The door had been open all night. So when I went in there on a Monday mornin' to sweep behind it, there was six-hundred-and eleven dollars layin' there. I t was paaay daaay. I didn't hang up a sign. Nobody never claimed it.

That bathroom was rough. Old Earl was here and I put some o' them green toilet deodorizer deals in the urinal. Beings as it was made o' fiber roof cement 'n stuff, they just stuck out there in that roof cement. It looked like that for years and them mints stayed in that urinal forever. It's still out there

Old Earl come in and said, "Hey Gary, somebody crapped in your urinal."

"Yeah they crapped in it, alright, that's for dam sure."

I eventually moved the bathroom to a one room unisex inside. It works better and I only have to change the toilet every year or so, or toilet tank, or a part once a year. It's not near as bad. I put a sink in the first one and they tore it off the wall before I got the line hooked up and the water workin'. I won't put a sink in it, so everyone uses Wet Ones, sanitary hand wipes. Out here in the desert I'm not puttin' a sink in that son-of-a-gun. They'll tear it off the wall. People will be fillin' five gallon water jugs in it. They'll be takin' baths in there left and right. Maintenance on it would break me.

I've seen 'em bathe in the back o' the toilet. I hope it's the back of the toilet. I mean they do it all the time. They'll go in the bathroom with dry hair and come out with wet hair. And there ain't no sink in there. What they do in toilets I cannot explain. My father told me when I bought this thing I'd really clean up. He didn't tell me it'd be vomit and feces and urine and other stuff I never wanted to see in my life. But you know it's better than the first day I was here when that truck pulled up and girls pee'd on one side 'n and the guys pee'd on the other side.

Chapter Fifty-Four
Success Without a Clue

A few years ago we had a Rainbow Convention. They all showed up down there 'bove Springerville. From what I could tell it was an excuse for a bunch o' hippies to git together, smoke dope and breathe Mother Nature's air and trash up the countryside. We had a couple of 'em stayed. Several of 'em stayed in the area. But we got one that stayed here at Witch Well. Loretta, a nature child.

I hired her old man, Carl, to work outside for me and Loretta was workin' for me inside. I needed some help patchin' roofs and whatever. So the day he worked for me . . . the *one* day, I'm up on the roof and he's down on the ground. Over on 'nother roof there's an extension ladder layin' there. Down on the ground there's a step ladder.

I yell at him, "Hey. Hand me up that extension ladder."

Now I was told this was a handy man. He could do all kinds o' things. He was buildin' him a house and stuff. He just stands there and looks at the two ladders.

He looks up at me and says, "Which one would that be?"

That was the one day that Carl worked for me. I had to explain everything to 'im. We were puttin' some roofin' on and I showed him a piece o' felt I was gonna use.

I'm gonna lay this felt up here and he says, "Now you need to explain this to me agin. Just how is this gonna work?"

And I said, "We're gonna do this, this, this, and this."

. He said, "OK. Now what do we do first?"

148

I put up with him one day. I wasn't there for him to have a conversation with himself over how to do it. I'm sure he built a nice snug house, for a handy-man who was buildin' a house, but I'm glad I missed out on that part. I'm sure Loretta had to help him 'long the way.

They were hippies dressed Reggae style. Dreadlock hair. Rainbow Child. Still live out here. Raise wolves.

Loretta wore cologne made from an oil called pachulie oil, whatever that is. She thought it smells good. Well, to me it smells like somebody ain't had a bath in a month. When she'd come to work it would just permeate the bar. I kept talkin' to her 'bout doin' her laundry and how she was livin' out there in the trees showerin' and stuff. I kept talkin' to her 'bout personal hygiene cause she's nice 'nough girl. She's honest on the till which means a lot. But I couldn't get over that smell. I thought she jist wasn't bathin'.

Finally one o' the deputy sheriffs told me what it was. I guess people use it cover up the smell o' marijuana or whatever they're usin'. To me, it's the most offensive stuff anybody could put on. I'd almost rather see a guy out whorin' covered in Old Spice so bad your eyes water than that stuff. Finally it was jist that pachulie that separated us. She couldn't work here anymore 'cause I got complaints from customers.

She told me, "Most people like it."

I said, "Who's most people? Nine out o' ten rainbow children? 'Cause the rest o' the world thinks that shit stinks."

She just kept wearin' it 'cause it was her. That's what she believed in wearin'. Said it was a natural fragrance. Well sure at thirty yards. Dirty ass is natural, too, but wash it. They may both be natural but you shouldn't take either one out into public.

After they quit workin' for me they went into the wolf business. Want to rescue the wolves. Well hell, if we want to bring back every critter on this country that's extinct, let's clone us back one o' them T-Rexes and turn him loose in Hollywood. Didn't they fall in that LaBrea Tar Pit or somthin'? Lets clone us in one o' them and turn 'im loose in their neighborhood.

The whole country thinks it's great to have wolves in my neighborhood. But they ain't got 'em in their neighborhood. Wolves are wolves. They're big opportunistic scavengers. And they'll kill. I think its fine to have 'em. I got nothin' 'gainst 'em. I'll tell you what, I think it's a cryin' shame in this country that I can go down to Phoenix and I can see a reward poster for a missin' child for five thousand dollars but here it's a hundred thousand dollar fine for killin' a wolf. America, where are your priorities?

I got nothin' 'gainst savin' a few wolves but the world has to realize that you're not gonna save 'em all. If you look, prob'ly twenty percent o' the wolves they turned out are missin'. There's a list o' missin' wolves as long as your arm. Wolves travel hundreds o' miles. You turn 'em out, no tellin' where they're gonna turn up. So any hundred thousand dollar fine on killin' a wolf is a ludicrous idea. Most people have never seen a wolf and wouldn't know one from a stray dog if it bit 'em.

Sheep herders'll kill stray dogs on sight. Ranchers'll kill stray dogs on sight. Stray dog the size of a wolf is gonna git shot sometime in life. He's gonna get run over. Mother Nature's gonna kill 'im. If a stray animal's after his herd, a rancher's not gonna ask it if he's a dog or a wolf. He's gonna protect his cattle and shoot.

The money we spend every day on them wolves is not fiscally responsible. I wish we would put that kind o' money into education. Into saving forests.

After Loretta left here and they got off on raisin' the wolves down there, they were puttin' 'em up signs on the fence along the highway. The state owns the fence and you can't jist go hang a billboard anywhere you want so the state took 'em down. I drive by one day and there's Loretta in the top of a tree. In the top of a cedar tree tryin' to hang a sign high enough out o' the right-o-way that the state boys couldn't take it down. What an idiot. I had to laugh. I've heard o' huggin a tree, but I thought you did it from the bottom.

They have survived though. As far as colorful forty-acre maggots, they fit right in. They work right in. They spent their first winter here in a pickup camper and that winter was cold. Three of 'em, Mom, Dad and their little girl. We saw ten below and they spent it in a pickup camper. They scratched a piece out o' this blow-sand and they're livin' on it. I give 'em credit for that.

Chapter Fifty-Five

Incoming

Debbie and I were sittin' here talkin' 'bout strange events and some o' the strange things we've seen comin' down this highway. A truck comes 'round the corner. We hear the truck gearin' down and all of a sudden KABOOM, this whole buildin' shakes. We walk outside and layin' 'gainst the buildin' is a steel ball the size of a bowlin' ball. Big old thing. Looks like a cannon ball and it'd rolled off that truck at probably fifty miles an hour and hit the buildin'.

We looked at that big old cannon ball and I said. "Run, Hon. Them Mormons are shootin' at us. I didn't know they had a gun that big. Twenty eight miles away, I thought we were safe."

Another time here comes a guy 'round the corner with a cross. He's got a couple o' four-by-fours. Eight footers and he's got 'em made into a cross. He's got a wheel on the bottom of it. He's walkin' 'cross the U.S. to go to Washington, D.C. from California as a religious statement. He's carryin' that cross like Jesus did.

One other time we got a guy comin' up the highway. We watched him for days come up the road there and the sheriff's department showed up. We all sat 'round and waited for 'im to come 'round the corner. He was dressed in prison stripes carryin' a ball and chain. He didn't think that over very well. Had 'im a big ol' ball and a chunk o' three-eights chain. Big ass chain 'round his ankle and he's carryin' that ball in a back pack. When he'd git to a town he'd show his chain. Out in here he had that chain from his ankle up to his back pack and had that ball in that back pack. He was walkin' 'cross the United States from California to the east coast to free all the political prisoners. Gonna demand freedom for all the unjustified prisoners in the United States.

Couple of 'em made local news. I've had several guys come through writin' books. The stories they tell about writin' books. Two of 'em were funny Lymies. Told me the only thing they learned 'bout Arizona is the only person without a gun is an ugly second grader that couldn't afford it yet.

Chapter Fifty-Six
Gun Control

In the state of Arizona, we're proud of our guns. We all have guns in Arizona. It'd be hard to take the guns away from your average Arizonan even though now-a-days most o' the average Arizonans are from Pennsylvania.

It used to be legal to bring 'em in a bar. I liked it 'cause I had some control over it. They'd bring 'em in and check 'em with me. I could tell how much they'd had to drink before I gave 'em back.

Then they outlawed bringin' 'em into a bar. Somebody come out here and sold somthin' like thirty-eight derringers in two weeks. Thirty-eight little guns. Piece-o'-shit little guns. 'Bout a month later we're sittin' in the sheriff's bar with him and his brother. There were a few of us sittin' at the bar and we're talkin' 'bout that new gun law, that you couldn't carry 'em in. One o' the guys reached down and pulled out a pistol and laid it on the bar. I reached down and pulled out a pistol and laid it on the bar. There were only 'bout five of us sittin' there and eight boot guns hit that damn bar. All the law did was make sure they hid 'em.

Before I had control over 'em. Now they're still here in this bar, I jist don't have any control over 'em anymore. Now they're hidden and this young generation, these young guys that wear them baggy clothes, they're packin', so it's gotten dicey. That law didn't help the bar business. Didn't help your average bar owner. Now I know there're certain idiots in the bar business that change these laws for all of us but I liked it better when they checked 'em with me than now.

Guns are a part of America. They're the reason we stood up with the colonialists and were able to hold off the British. They're the reason we carved this country out with settlers. They're a tool. One o' the greatest tools ever invented by man. The firearm. It has prob'ly done more to preserve civilization than anything else.

If you think 'bout one hundred thousand Incas bein' slaughtered in three days by swords and knives. If you think 'bout the way the Europeans killed with broad axes and blades, nothin' was more inhumane. Modern firearms are a pretty humane tool, when used in the right way. The day in history, in this country, that you can't own a gun will spell as the beginnin' of our downfall. The reason you can't whip us on this ground is the same reason they couldn't whip the colonials. Every one of us will come out and rise up. It may be the only time we come together, if we ever do. I don't know that we ever will.

I don't know that we ever will come together. But I kind o' believe the only thing that'll bring us together will be when the terrorists finally invade this soil. Gun laws deprivin' a citizen from protectin' 'imself; therefore also stops 'im from protectin' you. I'm a gun owner and I'm the same guy that goes and reads to the kindergarten. I'm the same guy that's Zero the Hero clown at the elementary school. I'm the guy you want on your side when everything goes to shit

My problem is that I truly believe it's not gonna happen for years, then I'm gonna be too damn old to enjoy it.

CHAPTER FIFTY-SEVEN
Mollycoddlin'

Takes a special kind o' guy to run one o' these state-line bars. I can't live in town. I was born and raised with Indians. I think like an Indian. In the days that I was raised in if you had trouble with a neighbor or you had trouble in the village or the town you were in, these arguments were settled with fists. Those arguments were settled with confrontation. They were settled violently. In town they use two-face and back-stabbin'. I can't live in town comfortably 'cause I think like an Indian. Out here, I'm not good surrounded by white folk.

I'm much more at ease. I'm much more myself when I'm surrounded by Native Americans. Most Native Americans are of good heart. These Pueblos that I deal with, these Zunis, I feel honored to be included as part o' their community. Whether they like me or not they're good people. Most native people are. They and those others of us who grow up amongst 'em think differently than people from white communities here in the west.

But I'm really 'fraid our country is gonna fall apart from the inside 'cause o' this stupidity over bigotry of any form. I know a lot 'bout racism. I was the only white guy in my high school. I grew up bouncin' from reservation to reservation. I was *belagana*, I was *washeechu*. I was *melayka*. I was always *the white kid*.

I never been 'round the black and white problem. I know it exists. I've seen it but it never existed with me. I never been 'round it but I have been 'round the red man/white man problem my whole life. And I don't have any answers. I don't care what color a person is. I do know it's silly.

It's absolutely silly. And 'til our country gets over that I don't know how we're ever gonna pull together.

Maybe nine-eleven pulled us closer than we've ever been but we have miles to go. I don't know how to reach the other generation. The counter culture, they have no fear. They're not 'fraid o' goin' to prison. That's three years with dental. That's a roof over your head every night. Hell that's your buddies hood. Half your bros are in there. We molly-coddled 'em in the eighties 'cause you couldn't spank your child. You couldn't discipline your child. CPS became a monster. That generation has no fear o' reprisal or consequences. They have no fear o' repercussion. They have no fear of anything they want to do.

I'm not sayin' all o' them are that way. But the numbers are staggerin'. The mentality is staggerin' and they've been created by liberal thinkin' on child raisin'. Dr. Spock did us no good. They've been sponsored by disdain for authority 'cause o' that. We created this monster. And when it goes to snot, I've got nothin' to say 'bout it.

Nothin ever gits settled. It's like the drive-by shootin's with the youth right now. In the old days we went out and knocked the snot outta each other and it was settled. It was over. Maybe come back in and have a beer together. Now they talk trash and they run for their piece. It's not the gun's fault. All they know is talk trash and shoot.

Well they shoot 'cause they're 'fraid to fight. 'Cause they don't know how to fight. They didn't grow up gittin' knocked 'round by their old man. They didn't grow up with a speed bag in the house. We grew up when fightin' was somethin' you had to do. I'm sure now they do, too. They gotta fight. They're over there fightin' by the time they're in the seventh grade. But by then they got a gun. They don't know what a gun's for. They just think it's for shootin' people. They've never had to go out and shoot a deer or shoot a rabbit or a squirrel so they can eat.

Chapter Fifty-Eight
Brilliance

See, I know how I'm gonna make my millions. I'm gonna build America's first drive-by shootin' range. I'm gonna build Americas first drive-by shootin' range for all those guys shootin' those innocent victims, shootin' guns on the street and whatever. They're shootin' people drivin' down the street holdin' a gun upside down. They don't know how to drive by and shoot.

So I'll build a drive-by shootin' range. You can build cardboard store fronts and you can put some guys in red bandanas and some guys in blue bandanas and a school bus down at the end o' the street. Then they can come here all the way from Phoenix. All the way from Phoenix and Tucson and Albuquerque.

We'll have a drive-by shoot-o-rama. We'll put it out there in the trees. We'll make us a course. Start red bandanas at one end, blue bandanas at another end, bring the long hair nuts in from one side and the skin heads from the other. Put out some cardboard cut-outs of a nurse and a couple school kids, ya know. Bring 'em all in the middle. Mix 'em up and let 'em learn to shoot whatever the hell they're aimin' at. Hell, they can't hit shit. Then, ya know, we could sell like nine-millimeters, and three-eighties, and the cheap ass ammo that they're usin'. They don't know how to use it. That's why they use so much of it. We could sell tickets at night, right up at the gate, make a little extra money.

If business got slow we can rent out the store fronts to store owners so they can learn to shoot back. 'Cause it's hard. You don't get no practice shootin' at movin' cars that's shootin' atcha. So we rent out store fronts to store owners so they can learn to shoot back at them guys drivin' by shootin' at 'em. Give 'em a chance to git in some practice.

America's first drive-by. I think it would sell millions. I think every Friday night it'd be lined up with low riders. Cause when they drive down the street, shootin' at people, they miss and kill an innocent child. They just don't git 'nough practice shootin' to know how to hit their target. That's where all our innocent victims are comin' from. If these guys had a drive by shootin' range then they could learn how to hit whoever the hell it is they're aimin' at.

Well all this TV shit has created all this. All them movies, all this holdin' the pistol upside down and all that. Well, OK, that's fine. I been there. I seen lead in the air. I looked down the barrel and seen it spit death. All that's a waste o' time.

You gotta calm down and hit what you're aimin' at or you're gonna die. These guys that're drivin' by, they'll be learnin' to shoot. Line up the lawyers outside waitin'. Yeah, I think its brilliant. America's first drive-by shoot-o-rama. Proceeds to go to unwed mothers.

Chapter Fifty-Nine
24-7-365

Gittin' rich. We all dream of it but what is rich? I don't have real extravagant taste. I guess to me rich would be to be able to afford what I wanted. Not have to work sixteen hours a day. I think if a guy had an eight-hour day job, weekends off and he didn't live too extravagantly and could afford a bottle whenever he wanted, that'd be rich, ya know.

Some people's perspective o' rich is different than mine. We all dream 'bout what would ya do. My idea would be that I'm gonna go somewhere where cows don't grow. I ain't never lived anywheres where cows didn't grow, ya know. My whole life I've stepped in cow shit in one form or another. Maybe own a lobster ranch er somethin'. I think rich is a state o' mind. I know guys who are filthy rich and they're the most miserable son-of-a-guns I've ever seen in my life.

I got a neighbor here who's got a big ranch. I mean a *big* ranch. He's got more money than he knows what to do with. He's jist got on 'nother fifteen million comin' his way. God is he rich. He's rich beyond rich to me and the guy lives alone. Sure he drives a rag top but he's seventy-eight years old and he's all alone. Some people say they don't care. They don't need anybody, they got all this money. What good does that do ya? Me, when I'm seventy-eight years old, got all that money, I think I'd be rich if I had one person I loved to share it with me. Do all those things with me. That would be rich.

People think I'm rich. I ain't rich. Long way from it. I pay my bills day by day, week by week like everybody else. I work sixteen-, twenty-hour days sometimes fifteen days straight, sometimes longer. My wife and I worked and never left this place for seven years. For seven years, seven days a week. Never left once. Finally left for one little bitty vacation after seven years and then never did it again for another four.

Chapter Sixty
I'm a Vegitarien

We're sittin' here workin' in the bar one time and two transvestites come in. Amongst Native Americans in this area we have a high number. Oh, I don't know what it's like 'round the world, but 'round here we git quite a few gays and homosexuals. I don't know what the percentage is but we got a bunch of 'em. My regular customers, who are homosexuals and gays, don't bother me a bit. Most o' the homosexuals are polite, clean, spend good money and cause very little problems.

I had two transvestites sittin' here one night. One of 'em was a pretty darn attractive man. He'd had the top half done but he didn't have the bottom half done yet (I assumed). One o' these little Zuni guys comes in and he jist falls in love with this bitch. He's buyin' it drinks and everything else, and gittin' the phone number off it and all that. Finally the crowd realizes that these aren't girls. These are guys even though one of 'em's got breasts, they're still guys.

The one with breasts sits down across the bar at me, looks deep into my eyes and says, "Gary, do you think I'm an attractive woman?"

I looked at 'im and said, "Ya know, with one or two more surgeries, I think you'll be there."

He says, "Oh thank you, Gary. I'm savin' up now to go to Trinidad."

Now in Trinidad, Colorado there's an old country doctor wears a cowboy hat and pushes Hereford cows. Evidently he's one o the best in the business at turnin' boys into girls. He makes 'em go up and live there a year. We've got one of 'em in Zuni that went up there and had the surgery done. Name used to be Daryl. but it's a girl now. Changed 'er name. Tiffany or somthin' like that.

Trinidad, Colorado ain't a place I'm ever gonna go to pick up girls in a bar 'cause that old doc he makes 'em live there as a woman for one year before he'll cut 'em. Queers from all over the world go to Trinidad, Colorado to git snipped. Oh yeeaah.

The other night we have a regular, Phillip, come in. Phillip's a good guy. I don't care that he's gay as hell. He's a pretty good guy and he don't flirt with me much and stuff. Those that flirt with me, I run 'em off. I don't put up with that much. I been in a pretty good mood sometimes, but I've never been gay. Well I walked out the other night and I'm trainin' a new bar maid and Carries's here so I went in and showered. Came back out after my shower and I didn't have my shirt buttoned all the way. Maybe the top two were open. I sat down and we were talkin'.

Finally Phillip looks at me and says, "Gary, did you shave your chest?"

Well, I been asked a lot o' things in my life but I never been asked if I shaved my chest before. The girls said I turned bright red and I'm sure I did.

I told 'im, "No. It took me fifty years to grow all seventeen o' these grey hairs and I'm not 'bout to shave 'em off."

Then we had 'nother one come in the same week, a Navajo boy. We got an assembly line set up. We're cuttin' meat. Carries's cuttin' into steaks and her girlfriend Cal's wrappin' meat. I got the hind quarters of a deer layin' on the bar, a few guys playin' pool, there's guys drinkin' beer. I like a bar where you're butcherin' deer, playin' pool and drinkin' beer all at the same time.

Well in comes this little gay guy. Walks right up to that hind quarter I'm cuttin' on with a knife. This little gay guy walks up to me and he says, "How much for your meat?" Well I've never been asked that before either.

I looked at 'im and I said, "I can't answer that question. Now if you were a woman, I could come up with a price. But for you I jist can't answer that question."

The whole place laughed 'im out the door.

One day I was shootin' pool and we had two of 'em in here and they were kind o' dancin' 'round the pool table. One of 'em had on lime green pants and the other had on bright raspberry colored pants. It got so every time I bent over to shoot pool, I could feel them two queers starin' at me. Finally I had to jist give up the pool game and go back 'round the bar where I felt safe.

Years ago, Dixie and Sue took me to a gay bar in Phoenix. I'd never been to a gay bar. We walked up to the door and there's a big old tall boy, bouncer, standin' there. When I walk up there I'm kind o' scruffy lookin'. Normal way o' dressin' for me.

He steps up to me and said, "You realize this is a gay bar?"

I said, "Well, no, I didn't realize that." He jist stands there and stares at me.

So I look at and I tell him, "Hey, Bud, I'm in a good mood. I'm not gay but I'm in a good mood."

He stepped back and he let me in. We went in there and set down and here come this little guy from 'round the corner. Got him a Stetson hat on. Got Wrangler pants creased down the front like we did back in the seventies. He was sure a cute little fella. He waited on me hand and foot all night. My beer never got empty, my ash tray never got full. He was jist right there tendin' to my every need. I had a helluva time in that bar. Dixie and I got up and danced. We were the only mixed couple on the dance floor and we drew a few looks but we didn't really care. So I partied 'til dam near closin' time in that queer bar and I never had a bit o' trouble. In fact I had some o' the best service I've ever had in my life. I never went back. 'Cause that woulda' been takin' it a little too far.

In here, one time, I got four or five o' my regular homosexuals and lesbians in the back room playin' pool. We got two new rednecks, come outta Montana, drivin' cows down there in the desert. Well they know it all but they're learnin' more quick. They might o' known it all when they got here and they might think they know it all, but they're learnin' quick. Welcome to the high desert plateau. Well they're in here one night havin' a couple o' beers and I got all my queers in the back room playin' pool, mindin' their own business.

These rednecks outta Montana take it personal that these gays are in here and they start runnin' their mouth. Finally I'd had 'nough. One of 'em mouthed off to one o' them regulars 'bout being queer.

I stepped up there and I said, "Hey, listen Bud, these are my fuckin' queers. You keep your mouth shut 'round my queers. If you wanna go somewhere else and raise hell with queers that's your business, but in this bar these are my queers and you keep your mouth shut. They are good customers. I'll throw your ass outta here before I'll throw their ass outta here."

Well right away these Montana rednecks figure I'm queer too but I'm not. I like women . . . more than they like me. When it comes to sexual preference, I'm a vaginaterian, I don't eat no meat.

Chapter Sixty-One
Desperate Aint Attractive

In high school, junior high, growin' up; girls didn't like me. Don Juan, I've never been. Never will be. I'm a little too rough 'round the edges. I'm a little scruffy. But as I've gotten older I've learned patience is a virtue. These good lookin' girls, they're sick and tired o' men chasin' 'em. They been pursued, harassed, and hounded since they were young girls. 'Specially out here in the west and on the reservation. Most o' the good lookin' girls got a baby by the time they're fifteen, sixteen-years old. They been messed with by grown men and stuff since they were young girls.

Desperate is never attractive. Now these guys come in this bar and there's a woman here and they're absolutely desperate. That runs them girls away. The hornier the guys are, the worse they are and them girls pick up on that right away. One o' the things I've learned 'bout attractive women is you jist leave 'em 'lone. If they want you, they'll come to ya. If you harass 'em, you ain't gonna git nowhere. So you jist sit back with a sense o' humor, be quiet and polite and they'll come your way when they're ready. There ain't no sense in chasin' 'em 'cause all you'll do is chase 'em off. It's like huntin' elk. If you chase 'em and harass 'cm, they're gonna leave the country. They ain't gonna come back. If you jist sit back and bide your time, they'll come to ya. Good-lookin' women aren't much different than an elk.

Chapter Sixty-Two
Keepin' Goin'

Here's a little glimpse on how I cope with the challenges of life. One is for Larry, a friend I recently lost. One is for a friend I never will.

You're six miles from town
With a trailer breakin' down,
Haulin' a loco cow, snubbed in a haze.
It's just another one of those days.

You've got 2 flats on an open top,
And you know darn well that critter will climb if you stop.

No cell phone to call in,
Much to mamma's chagrin,
Thinkin' of quittin' this job,
If you can't clear that next knob,
It'd be a little easier walk in.

You give a quick prayer, another tire doesn't pop.
Catch a glimpse of the house, as you crawl to the top,
With a mile and a half to go,
Hear that third tire blow.
Still you press on in,
Giving' up on savin' tire and rim.

Get to the corral to unload,
Feeling beat, tired and rode.
Back up to put her inside,
Step out of the truck with a limp in your stride,
You discover the ol' girl has died.
It tugs on your heart and drags on your pride,

You've been shit at and missed,
Kicked at and hit.
Shake your head and say,
Tomorrow's another day.

Motherin' these cows,
You're never gonna quit.
You and the lord,
Wouldn't have it any other way.

Debra Sue she flew.
That Sunday back in '82
How long that flight would last I never knew.
I think it will be with us till 2032.

Off the back of the Harley she flew straight and true,
Just missed the light post onto the grass covered in dew.
It was my fault; God knows that's true,
I lost focus when those church dresses flew.

As they exited the house of the almighty,
The Lord's breath lifted their skirts lightly.
My attention drifted from the road more than slightly,
It was too late when she screamed and grabbed tightly.

The car appeared in my sight, after running a red light,
I laid that scooter down, in that dirty Denver town.
When I last looked it was a green light,
As I tried to avoid the crash with all my might.

Under the bumper I slid, without leather or skid lid,
Debra Sue, she flew clear out of sight.
That cage burned rubber as it took off in flight.

As the asphalt devoured my meat and skin,
To count my blessings, I can't begin.
The soft grass caught her just scuffing her knees and chin
Looking at skirts with one on the back,
I'll never do again.
Thank-you Lord for pointing out the cost of sin,
'Cause when that story comes up, I never win

Chapter Sixty-Three
Drawin' the Line

Sex is a big part o' the bar business. I don't care what any bar owner says. Well, maybe their bars are different, but in my bar sex is a big part o' the business. People dream 'bout it, they talk 'bout it, they try to practice it, they try to do anything they can with sex. I'm sure when you bring alcohol into the situation it lowers people's inhibitions.

Men pull it out and pee in the parkin' lot, jist pull it out and pee. Some of 'em, while I'm waitin' on 'em at the drive-up window, stand up and pee on the side o' the buildin' while they're talkin' to me.

I always try to give 'em a come back, ya know. "Damn. If my dick was that small I wouldn't bring it out in public." I give 'em hell for doin' things like that.

These Zunis are the horniest people I've ever been 'round in my life. It's all they think 'bout. Over many years here, sex is a constant topic.

Had a guy sittin' in here the other day and he said, "Gary, they're talkin' 'bout you in Zuni."

I said, "So?"

He said, "Really. They're talkin' 'bout you in Zuni."

I said, "They been talkin' 'bout me in Zuni for twenty years. Ain't nothin new 'bout that." "What're they sayin'?"

He says, "They're sayin' you're a yellow-bellied sap sucker."

Now from the school I grew up in that's a fist fight so it kind o' tightens my jaw a little bit. I sit there and finally he keeps talkin' that

I'm a yellow-bellied sap sucker and everybody in here has kind o' got a quizzical look on their face. Nobody knows what he's talkin' 'bout.

Finally he asked me, "Do you know what a yellow-bellied sap sucker is?"

I said, "Yeah. I know what a yellow-bellied sap sucker is. It's a bird 'bout the size of a meadow lark, got a yellow belly on him, got a long beak. Yeah, I know what a yellow-bellied sap sucker is."

He says, "No. That's not what I mean."

I said, "Then just what the hell do you mean that I'm a yellow-belly sap sucker?"

He says, "You eat pussy." Oh my god the place breaks up. I start, laughin' at 'im.

I said, "If that's what you're talkin' 'bout, then you're damn right. I'm the Mozart o' the muff divers. I'm an ar-teest. I can hum the Battle Hymn o' the Republic. I give lessons to lesbians on Tuesday and Thursday nights. If that's what they're talkin' 'bout, that I eat pussy, you go back and tell 'em I'm a fuckin' Rembrandt."

The whole place jist cracked up 'cause nobody knew what the hell he was talkin' 'bout. He was jist tryin' to git me ruffled, or whatever. He was jist makin' up a story so he could tell his joke. Sometimes they jist try to see what they can do to git me, to make me react.

When we're in a combative situation and they give me the fuck you, I tell 'em, "Well if you ever did fuck me you'd give up sheep. If you ever did fuck me, you wouldn't walk for two weeks. You ever did fuck me, you'd never go back to your sister."

I give 'em all kinds o' hell when they give me that F. U. When they wanna fight and you make fun out of 'em and everybody's laughin' at 'em nine times out o' ten they won't fight. They jist git embarrassed and leave.

I got an ex-wife, sex with her was great. I jist hated standin' in line for my turn. Green-eyed, black-haired girl. Just a doll years ago; like we all were years ago. The meanest bitch that ever walked.

Cold as they come. I tried to git her on a government program after we got divorced. She was whinin' 'bout money so I got her on a government program. I can't tell you how cold this bitch was. They sent her down to the equator to see if she could slow global warming. She was there a couple o' months and the temperature o' the world dropped a couple o' degrees and the Ecuadorian divorce rate went up six-hundred-percent. They deported 'er back. There's a federal mandate now that we can't live within' five western states of each other.

I have a good partner that got with a new woman. She was a little bit racist. We're drinkin' one night and she gits in on me 'bout Custer and everything. She was gittin' kind o' racist on me, ya know. Finally she gives me the F.U. 'cause I'm obstinate. When I git a few drinks in me I'm an obstinate son-of-a-gun. I git loud and I'm opinionated. Finally she's had 'nough o' my loud opinionated ass. She gives me the F.U.

I look at 'er with my buddy sittin' right next to me and I said, "Hell, Bitch, I wouldn't do you with *his* dick. I like 'im bettern' that."

Her only comeback was, "Well, I wouldn't do you with his dick either."

He and I looked at each other. Neither one of us were interested in that.

Chapter Sixty-Four
Beneficial Loss

My old partner, he had a wife disappear on 'im. Best thing ever happened to 'im. It was hard on the kids 'cause when your mother just leaves, never comes back, never calls, never sends a Christmas card, you never know what happened to her. That makes it hard on the kids but as far as Russ goes, it's the best thing ever happened to 'im. Last we heard, she was wrattlin' chicken bones down in the bayou or somethin'. She was always a crystal carryin', metaphysical misfit anyway.

After she left, ol' Russ went through a few girlfriends. We were a little worried 'bout 'im 'cause them girlfriends were Awful Alma, Scary Sherry, and Terrible Tina. He liked those psycho girls. For some reason he was attracted to psycho bitches. I never have been. Those girls'll slit ya.

When she run off and left Russ the youngest, was 'bout fifteen. The other boys were already on their own. All three o' them boys have worked for me over the years. The oldest one, he was workin' for me one day and I was chewin' on him for bein' lazy. He said, "Well, why? It doesn't matter. I'm never gonna work for a livin'."

"What the hell you gonna do?"

"I'm just gonna deal drugs. Gonna deal drugs for a livin."

"That's one o' the stupidest things I've ever heard from a man who has to learn to work."

He said, "You can jist go to hell."

"I know I'm goin' there. I'm goin' into middle level management. What you gotta worry 'bout is when you git there I'm still your boss. When you git to hell, they're gonna give you a damn shovel and I'm gonna be standin' there with a whip. Goin' to hell don't scare me one bit."

When I finally die I'm gonna ketch up on my sleep. I look forward to it. Dyin' don't scare me. Sometimes I'm 'fraid of livin'. Sometimes the things I have to do and the compromises I have to make bother me far worse than the thought o' dyin' does.

When you git in a real dangerous situation, dyin' don't enter your mind. People talk 'bout the desire for survival takes over. That may be the case but I've been in a few o' those death-defyin' situations and dyin' don't enter your mind. Survival don't enter your mind 'cause your mind is *I have to do this next. This is what I have to do.* You don't think 'bout livin' or dyin' or any o' that. Maybe that's what the survival instinct is. I don't know.

The middle boy, he worked for me for a while till he got to stealin'. Bad. See, it's hard to catch thieves in the bar business if you're not here twenty-four hours a day watchin' 'em with cameras and tapes. I got cameras 'round and stuff but I think it's imposin'. I think it's a little twisted to sit and watch your employees on monitors. There's somethin' wrong with that. And if you have to sit and watch 'em 'cause you don't trust 'em you're better off jist firin' 'em. Git rid of 'em. It's not worth your time.

When I caught the middle one stealin', I'd been leavin' 'bout ten o'clock at night or so pretty regular, and goin' into town to see my wife. I left one night 'bout eleven. I told 'im I was leavin' and I got me a six pack; then I headed for town. Well I didn't head for town. I jist went down the road a little ways and pulled into my cow pasture 'n shut the lights off and come up through the trees and set over there in the trees and had a couple o' beers and watched 'im. After he figured I was gone for a while, then there he was haulin' cases o' beer outta the back o' my cooler into the back o' his car. He thought he was safe 'cause I had set up a pattern o' goin' into town and leavin' 'im alone on Friday and Saturday nights. So he had his own little bootleggin' side business goin' on haulin' beer into town. That trap worked.

Chapter Sixty-Five
100% American

I'm Irish and English and German mix. Now as far as me bein' white, I'm not white. I'm non-pigmentation challenged. You put me out in the sun, I can be brown, I can be tan, I can be bright red. You git me sick, I can be green, gray, yellow. I can be all kinds o' colors. So I'm not really a white boy, I'm jist non-pigmentation challenged. I can be any color o' the rainbow. All this conversation about me bein' a white boy, they've got no idea what it's like to change color. I do with every season. We git those racist comments every now and again.

Carrie, my favorite barmaid, right now, and has been for five or six years, has a wonderful sense o' humor. One time we were workin' on a Sunday, no, I guess it was a Saturday night. A girl comes in the door with a beer in her hand. Well it's illegal to walk in a bar and bring your own drink so old Carrie told her she had to go back outside. She went back outside and threw her beer in the parkin' lot and came back in.

Came up to us and Carrie told her, "Naw. I'm sorry. You've had too much. I can't serve you."

Now Carrie's a large girl. She's a large woman and she's real dark complected. Native American Zuni as dark as any of 'em and this woman, she asked if Carrie's my daughter.

I hug old Carrie and say, "Yeah, she's my daughter." The woman keeps askin' for alcohol. We keep tellin' her no.

Finally she turns on me and says, "You're a racist."

I don't know how she thinks I could be a racist with this daughter. While we're huggin' there she believes I'm a racist.

I ask her, "What kind o' racist would I be if I had a daughter that looked like this?"

The old girl jist keeps gittin' madder 'n madder 'n madder. Finally she got to the door and turns and says she's gonna have her vatos come back and git me. Then she gave me the F.U.

I told her, "Bitch, I wouldn't do you with your own dildo."

Chapter Sixty-Six

Complaint

I have a wealth o' happiness. I'm the luckiest man in the world. I got to come back to where I spent my childhood. And make a livin'. Make a good livin'. It's been hard, yeah, but I git to hunt deer where I killed my first deer thirty-seven years ago. I git to live where I have roots. I git to live here in peace 'cause I'm at peace with myself. And I guess they're right, I am rich. I enjoy life. When they bury my sorry butt no one out there can say I didn't enjoy life. I've gone down lots o' good roads.

I've had all kinds o' jobs. I put trailer houses together. I moved houses, I worked in hardware stores, I built power lines, I built buffalo fence, poured concrete, worked in clothing. I've gone 'round a lot. but I'm truly at home here in Witch Well, Arizona. When I was a little kid comin' down here are some o' the fondest memories o' my childhood.

Some fondest memories o' my childhood was in Eagle Butte. Wasn't any drinkin' water there that was worth a damn. So we went to a spring clear out there on the Cheyenne River to git drinkin' water every week. That's where I learned to shoot a shotgun, hunt prairie dogs. That's where I learned how grouse fly, where mule deer go and that's where I learned much o' my early sportsmanship. Those are good things. To be able to come back and make a livin' where you learned those things is lucky.

Some o' those guys that come in out here are just so outta place. Each to his own and all that but even out here in the middle o' nowhere we see a bit o' what you guys see in the city. I mean the crazy stuff. People dressed all in scarves o' six different colors, the hair and studded eyelids.

We see that stuff. Everybody wants to be noticed I guess. I've always wanted to be unnoticed. I'm the kind o' guy who wants to sit back and watch. I don't like to be up front. I will go up front when called upon. But I don't like to be up there.

The only compliment I ever got 'bout being up front was this year. We buried a biker outta Zuni. He wrecked on this highway down the road a little way. Killed 'im. We had a little memorial service at the south end o' the ranch. I hadn't done much like that in my life but at the service I figured we needed a little o' the Lord's influence that wasn't there. They were mainly bikers and there wasn't a touch o' the Lord in there so I stepped in and I sang *Amazing Grace*. Then we put out a feed here at the bar afterwards for the guy and stuff. Two o' them biker girls come up to me and told me I had a wonderful voice.

I told 'em, "Sure, I finally get a compliment and it's outta two bitches been on the back of a Harley for twenty-years who can't hear nothin' anyway."

I do have a distinctive voice. It has been to my advantage in here. A good friend o' mine, Kay Tinnen, he's a cowboy lives over in Zuni. He told me that one o' my biggest advantages in this bar is when I get mad everybody knows it. My voice resonates throughout the room and it's intimidatin'. It has been one o' my favorite weapons. If I can psyche a guy out and not have to fight 'im I'll do it every time. If I can scare the hell out o' him without havin' to punch 'im you know, that's a win. I do it a lot. I am what I say. What comes outta my mouth is over-powerin' for 'em so I use it a lot. It's the best tool I can use to diffuse the problem.

Chapter Sixty-Seven
Standards

Thing is, I'm overbearin'. When I like someone I'm not. When I don't like someone then I am. I have survived out here, and in my life, I guess, by a certain machismo facade. Got no choice. When shots are fired, people need to know you're in charge, that they have someone they can trust to take care o' things.

I have to wear many different hats out here. First aid on highway rescues, fightin' fire, car wrecks, strange situations. People in dire need and people that are on the swindle. Strange situations. A timid man can't do this job.

Wendell used a pistol. I use my voice. I bark and I bite. I try to use only that force necessary to defuse the situation and then remove myself from it as quickly as I can. I've prob'ly been over-physical at times, but never used more than that force I deem necessary to handle the situation. Sometimes that force is great and vicious.

I learned early in life never hit a man while he's down. It's easier to kick 'im.